WOK

MW01255805

Cookbook

© Copyright 2019. Laura Sommers.
All rights reserved.
No part of this book may be reproduced in any form or by any electronic or
mechanical means without written permission of the author. All text,
illustrations and design are the exclusive property of
Laura Sommers

Introduction

The wok is a essential tool in any Asian kitchen or any kitchen that aspires to cooking asian cuisine. The wok, with it's curved design creates a focal point at the bottom of the pan which helps to regulate the heat and traps the flavor. Although many dishes can be made in a traditional western skillet, many would argue that it does not produce the same flavorful results as a wok.

Many different cooking techniques can be done in a wok, including stir frying, steaming, pan frying, deep frying, poaching, boiling, braising, searing, stewing, making soup, smoking and roasting nuts.

This cookbook contains a delicious varieties of recipes to be made using the wok.

Beef Lo Mein

Ingredients:

1 (8 oz.) package spaghetti
1 tsp. dark sesame oil
1 tbsp. peanut oil
4 cloves garlic, minced
1 tbsp. minced fresh ginger root
4 cups mixed vegetables
1 pound flank steak, thinly sliced
3 tbsps. soy sauce
2 tbsps. brown sugar
1 tbsp. oyster sauce
1 tbsp. Asian chile paste with garlic

Directions:

1. Bring a large pot of lightly salted water to a boil.
2. Cook spaghetti in the boiling water until cooked through but firm to the bite, about 12 minutes; drain and transfer to a large bowl. Drizzle sesame oil over the spaghetti; toss to coat.
3. Place a plate atop the bowl to keep the noodles warm.
4. Heat peanut oil in a wok over medium-high heat.
5. Cook and stir garlic and ginger in hot oil until fragrant, about 30 seconds.
6. Add mixed vegetables to the wok; cook and stir until slightly tender, about 3 minutes.
7. Stir flank steak into the vegetable mixture; cook and stir until the beef is cooked through, about 5 minutes.
8. Mix soy sauce, brown sugar, oyster sauce, and chile paste together in a small bowl; pour over the spaghetti. Dump spaghetti and sauce mixture into the wok with the vegetables and steak; cook and stir until the spaghetti is hot, 2 to 3 minutes.

Tsao Mi Fun (Taiwanese Fried Rice Noodles)

Ingredients:

1/2 pound thinly sliced pork loin
1/4 cup soy sauce
1/4 cup rice wine
1 tsp. white pepper
1 tsp. Chinese five-spice powder
1 tsp. cornstarch
4 dried Chinese black mushrooms
1 (8 oz.) package dried rice vermicelli
1/4 cup vegetable oil, divided
2 eggs, beaten
1/4 clove garlic, minced
1 tbsp. dried small shrimp
3 carrots, cut into matchstick strips
1/2 onion, chopped
3 cups bean sprouts
4 leaves napa cabbage, thinly sliced
Salt to taste
3 sprigs fresh cilantro for garnish

Directions:

1. Place the pork into a mixing bowl and pour in the soy sauce and rice wine.
2. Sprinkle with the white pepper, five-spice powder, and cornstarch.
3. Mix well, then set aside to marinate. Soak the mushrooms in a bowl of cold water for 20 minutes, then pour off the water, cut off and discard the stems of the mushrooms.
4. Slice the mushrooms thinly and reserve. Soak the rice vermicelli in a separate bowl of cold water for 10 minutes, then pour off the water and set the noodles aside.
5. Heat 1 tbsp. of the vegetable oil in a wok over medium heat.
6. Pour in the eggs, and cook until firm, flipping once, to make a pancake.
7. Remove the egg pancake, and allow to cool, then thinly slice and place into a large bowl. Heat 2 more tbsps. of the vegetable oil in the wok over high heat.
8. Stir in the garlic and dried shrimp, and cook until the shrimp become aromatic, about 20 seconds. Next, add the pork along with the marinade, and cook until the pork is no longer pink, about 4 minutes.
9. Stir in the carrots and onion, and cook until the carrots begin to soften, about 3 minutes.
10. Finally, add the bean sprouts, napa cabbage, and sliced mushrooms; cook and stir until the vegetables are tender, about 3 minutes more.

11. Scrape the pork mixture into the bowl along with the eggs, then wipe out the wok and return it to the stove over medium-high heat.
12. Heat the remaining vegetable oil in the wok, then stir in the drained rice vermicelli noodles.
13. Cook and stir for a few minutes until the noodles soften, then stir in the reserved pork mixture. Scrape the mixture in to a serving bowl and garnish with cilantro to serve.

Chinese Buffet Green Beans

Ingredients:

1 tbsp. oil, peanut or sesame
2 cloves garlic, thinly sliced
1 pound fresh green beans, trimmed
1 tbsp. white sugar
2 tbsps. oyster sauce
2 tsps. soy sauce

Directions:

1. Heat peanut oil in a wok over medium-high heat.
2. Stir in the garlic, and cook until the edges begin to brown, about 20 seconds.
3. Add the green beans; cook and stir until the green beans begin to soften, about 5 minutes.
4. Stir in the sugar, oyster sauce, and soy sauce. Continue cooking and stirring for several minutes until the beans have attained the desired degree of tenderness.

Balsamic Vinegar and Ginger Bok Choy

Ingredients:

4 heads baby bok choy
3 tbsps. olive oil
1/4 cup water
2 tbsps. capers
1 1/2 tsps. minced garlic
1 1/2 tsps. minced fresh ginger root
2 tbsps. balsamic vinegar
1 dash fresh lemon juice, or to taste

Directions:

1. Separate the leaves from the stems of the bok choy.
2. Cut the stems into bite-sized chunks and shred the leaves.
3. Heat the olive oil in a wok over medium heat.
4. Cook the bok choy stems in the oil until slightly tender, about 3 minutes; add the water and leaves and cook until the water evaporates, about 10 minutes more.
5. Stir in the capers, garlic, and ginger; cook and stir 1 minute more.
6. Sprinkle the vinegar and lemon juice over the bok choy and remove from heat; serve immediately.

Honey-Ginger Shrimp and Vegetable

Ingredients:

2 tbsps. olive oil
3 cloves garlic, minced
1/2 onion, chopped
1 1/2 tsps. ground ginger
2 tsps. red pepper flakes
1 red bell pepper, chopped
1/2 zucchini, halved lengthwise and sliced
3 cups fresh mushrooms, coarsely chopped
2 tbsps. cornstarch
1/2 cup honey
1 pound medium shrimp - peeled and deveined
Salt and pepper to taste

Directions:

1. Heat olive oil in a wok over high heat until it begins to smoke.
2. Stir in garlic, onion, ginger, and red pepper flakes. Quickly cook until the onion softens and just begins to brown.
3. Stir in bell pepper, zucchini, and mushrooms; continue cooking until the zucchini softens, about 4 minutes.
4. Stir cornstarch into honey until smooth, then add to vegetables, and simmer until thickened, about 2 minutes.
5. Add shrimp, and cook until they turn pink, about 3 minutes.
6. Season to taste with salt and pepper before serving.

Thai Spicy Basil Chicken Fried Rice

Ingredients:

3 tbsps. oyster sauce
2 tbsps. fish sauce
1 tsp. white sugar
1/2 cup peanut oil for frying
4 cups cooked jasmine rice, chilled
6 large cloves garlic clove, crushed
2 serrano peppers, crushed
1 pound boneless, skinless chicken breast, cut into thin strips
1 red pepper, seeded and thinly sliced
1 onion, thinly sliced
2 cups sweet Thai basil
1 cucumber, sliced (optional)
1/2 cup cilantro sprigs (optional)

Directions:

1. Whisk together the oyster sauce, fish sauce, and sugar in a bowl.
2. Heat the oil in a wok over medium-high heat until the oil begins to smoke.
3. Add the garlic and serrano peppers, stirring quickly.
4. Stir in the chicken, bell pepper, onion and oyster sauce mixture.
5. Cook until the chicken is no longer pink.
6. Raise heat to high and stir in the chilled rice; stir quickly until the sauce is blended with the rice. Use the back of a spoon to break up any rice sticking together.
7. Remove from heat and mix in the basil leaves. Garnish with sliced cucumber and cilantro as desired.

Ginger Veggie Stir-Fry

Ingredients:

1 tbsp. cornstarch1
1/2 cloves garlic, crushed
2 tsps. chopped fresh ginger root, divided
1/4 cup vegetable oil, divided
1 small head broccoli, cut into florets
1/2 cup snow peas
3/4 cup julienned carrots
1/2 cup halved green beans
2 tbsps. soy sauce
2 1/2 tbsps. water
1/4 cup chopped onion
1/2 tbsp. salt

Directions:

1. In a large bowl, blend cornstarch, garlic, 1 tsp. ginger, and 2 tbsps. vegetable oil until cornstarch is dissolved.
2. Mix in broccoli, snow peas, carrots, and green beans, tossing to lightly coat.
3. Heat remaining 2 tbsps. oil in a wok over medium heat.
4. Cook vegetables in oil for 2 minutes, stirring constantly to prevent burning.
5. Stir in soy sauce and water.
6. Mix in onion, salt, and remaining 1 tsp. ginger.
7. Cook until vegetables are tender but still crisp.

Panang Curry with Chicken

Ingredients:

5 tbsps. Panang curry paste
Cooking oil
4 cups coconut milk
2/3 pound skinless, boneless chicken breast, cubed
2 tbsps. palm sugar
2 tbsps. fish sauce, or to taste
6 kaffir lime leaves, torn
2 fresh red chile peppers, sliced
1/4 cup fresh Thai basil leaves

Directions:

1. Fry the curry paste in the oil in a wok over medium heat until fragrant.
2. Stir the coconut milk into the curry paste and bring to a boil.
3. Add the chicken; cook and stir until the chicken is nearly cooked through, 10 to 15 minutes.
4. Stir the palm sugar, fish sauce, and lime leaves into the mixture; simmer together for 5 minutes. Taste and adjust the saltiness by adding more fish sauce if necessary. Garnish with sliced red chile peppers and Thai basil leaves to serve.

Moo Goo Gai Pan

Ingredients:

1 tbsp. vegetable oil
1 cup sliced fresh mushrooms
2 cups chopped broccoli florets
1 (8 oz.) can sliced bamboo shoots, drained
1 (8 oz.) can sliced water chestnuts, drained
1 (15 oz.) can whole straw mushrooms, drained
1 tbsp. vegetable oil
2 cloves garlic, minced
1 pound skinless, boneless chicken breast, cut into strips
1 tbsp. cornstarch
1 tbsp. white sugar
1 tbsp. soy sauce
1 tbsp. oyster sauce
1 tbsp. rice wine
1/4 cup chicken broth

Directions:

1. Heat 1 tbsp. of vegetable oil in a wok over high heat until it begins to smoke.

2. Stir in the fresh mushrooms, broccoli, bamboo shoots, water chestnuts, and straw mushrooms.
3. Cook and stir until all the vegetables are hot, and the broccoli is tender, about 5 minutes.
4. Remove from the wok, and set aside. Wipe out the wok.
5. Heat the remaining tbsp. of vegetable in the wok until it begins to smoke.
6. Stir in the garlic, and cook for a few seconds until it turns golden-brown.
7. Add the chicken, and cook until the chicken has lightly browned on the edges, and is no longer pink in the center, about 5 minutes.
8. Stir together the cornstarch, sugar, soy sauce, oyster sauce, rice wine, and chicken broth in a small bowl.
9. Pour over the chicken, and bring to a boil, stirring constantly. Boil for about 30 seconds until the sauce thickens and is no longer cloudy. Return the vegetables to the wok, and toss with the sauce.

Orange Ginger Shrimp Stir-Fry

Ingredients:

1 pound peeled, deveined shrimp
2 tbsps. orange juice
1 tsp. minced garlic
1 tsp. minced fresh ginger root
Salt and ground black pepper, to taste
1 tbsp. vegetable oil
1 tbsp. sesame oil
1 tbsp. vegetable oil
1 green bell pepper, diced
1 yellow summer squash, sliced
1 cup chopped broccoli
1/2 cup diced onion
1/2 cup chopped carrot
1 orange, zested
1/4 tsp. cayenne pepper
1 1/2 cups cooked rice (optional)

Directions:

1. Stir shrimp, orange juice, garlic, and ginger together in bowl; season with salt and pepper. Refrigerate 15 minutes.
2. Heat 1 tbsp. vegetable oil and sesame oil in a wok over medium-high heat.
3. Remove shrimp from the marinade; cook and stir in the hot oil until opaque, about 2 minutes per side. Transfer shrimp to a plate.
4. Heat 1 tbsp. vegetable oil with the oil remaining in the wok.
5. Cook and stir bell pepper, squash, broccoli, onion, carrot, orange zest, and cayenne pepper in the hot oil until the vegetables are tender, about 5 minutes. Return shrimp to the wok, stir into the vegetable mixture, and continue cooking 1 minute more.

Wok Chicken Wings

Ingredients:

12 to 15 chicken wings cut at joints and tips removed
2 tbsp. soy sauce
2 tbsp. Chinese cooking wine
1/2 tsp. five spice
Peanut or Wok oil
4 slices fresh ginger root (thinly cut)
2 cloves garlic crushed
1/4 cup sugar
1/2 cup water
1 tbsp. Lite soya sauce

Directions:

1. On high heat, add oil, garlic and ginger root to Wok.
2. Cook, stirring for 1 to 2 minutes.
3. Add chicken pieces and continue to move mixture in Wok for 1 to 2 minutes.
4. Add remaining ingredients (mix these together and add as a fluid mixture).
5. Put to medium heat, cover and stir occasionally for 30 to 45 minutes.
6. Cook until only oil is left in bottom of wok. Serve as finger food, or with rice on the side for an entree.

Indonesian Fried Rice (Nasi Goreng)

Ingredients:

1 cup uncooked white rice
2 cups water cooking spray
3 eggs, beaten
1 tbsp. vegetable oil
1 onion, chopped
1 leek, chopped
1 clove garlic, minced
2 green chile peppers, chopped
1/2 pound chicken breasts, cut into thin strips
1/2 pound peeled and deveined prawns
1 tsp. ground coriander
1 tsp. ground cumin
3 tbsps. sweet soy sauce (Indonesian kecap manis)

Directions:

1. Bring the rice and water to a boil in a saucepan over high heat.
2. Reduce heat to medium-low, cover, and simmer until the rice is tender, and the liquid has been absorbed, 20 to 25 minutes.
3. Spread onto a baking sheet, and refrigerate 2 hours until cold.
4. Heat a large nonstick wok over medium heat. Spray with nonstick cooking spray.
5. Pour eggs into hot wok.
6. Cook until the eggs begin to set, lifting up the edges of the set eggs to allow the uncooked egg to contact the hot pan, about 1 minute. Flip omelet in one piece and cook until fully set, about 30 seconds.
7. Slice omelet into 1/2 inch strips.
8. Heat the vegetable oil in a wok or large frying pan over high heat.
9. Stir in the onion, leek, garlic, and chile peppers.
10. Cook, stirring, until onion is soft, 3 to 5 minutes.
11. Stir in the chicken, prawns, coriander, and cumin, mixing well.
12. Cook and stir for approximately 5 minutes.
13. Mix in the cold rice, sweet soy sauce, and omelet strips; cook until shrimp are bright pink and chicken is no longer pink in the center, 3 to 5 minutes.

Cabbage In A Wok

Ingredients:

1 lg. cabbage
1 lg. onion
2 lg. carrots
2 lg. white potatoes
1 tbsp. oil
1 tbsp. sugar or to taste
Salt and pepper to taste
1 cup water
2 slices fat back or favorite meat seasoning

Directions:

1. Cut up cabbage and rinse with water, then let drain. Do not shake off water. Chop the onion, slice carrots thin, and then slice the potatoes. Leave potatoes in water until ready to use.
2. Heat wok (350 degrees).
3. Add in oil with 2 slices of fat back meat or any other seasoning meat. Let it cook in the oil for about 2 to 3 minutes.
4. Add the chopped onion and carrots. Let cook until onions are clear.
5. Add cabbage, stir around to cover with oil, let cook for 15 minutes, stirring occasionally.
6. Sprinkle with sugar, salt and pepper to taste.
7. Add enough water to keep cabbage from burning. Do not over cook cabbage (crisp). When just about done, place the potato slices on top of cabbage and cover until done.

Chicken Tarragon In A Wok

Ingredients:

2 tsp. seasoned salt
1/4 tsp. black pepper
Dash of paprika
1 (2 1/2 to 3 lb.) broiler chicken (cut up into small pieces)
1/4 cup olive oil
1 med./large onion thinly sliced
10 fresh mushrooms, sliced
1 tsp. dried tarragon
1/4 cup water

Directions:

1. Combine first 3 ingredients; sprinkle over (or rub into) chicken. Brown chicken slowly in olive oil in wok; remove from wok. Saute onions and mushrooms in some olive oil in wok. Move onions and mushrooms aside and place chicken back in wok. Spoon onions, mushrooms and tarragon over chicken.
2. Add water, cover and simmer until chicken is tender (18 to 20 minutes). Use remaining liquid as gravy over rice.
3. Makes 4 to 6 servings.

Tomato and Egg Stir Fry

Ingredients:

2 tbsps. avocado oil, or as needed
6 eggs, beaten
4 ripe tomatoes, sliced into wedges
2 green onions, thinly sliced

Directions:

1. Heat 1 tbsp. avocado oil in a wok over medium heat.
2. Cook and stir eggs in the hot oil until mostly cooked through, about 1 minute. Transfer eggs to a plate.
3. Pour remaining 1 tbsp. avocado oil into wok; cook and stir tomatoes until liquid has mostly evaporated, about 2 minutes. Return eggs to wok and add green onions; cook and stir until eggs are fully cooked, about 30 more seconds.

Apple Fried Rice

Ingredients:

6 oz. shrimp - peeled, veined, and cut into 1-inch pieces
1 pinch salt
Ground black pepper to taste
1 tsp. cornstarch
1 tbsp. vegetable oil, or more as needed
1 tsp. minced garlic
1 egg, beaten
1 cup diced button mushrooms
3/4 cup frozen mixed vegetables
1 apple - peeled, cored, and diced
2 tbsps. raisins
1 tsp. curry powder
1 tbsp. light soy sauce
2 cups overnight steamed white rice
1 green onion, diced

Directions:

1. Mix shrimp, salt, and pepper together in a bowl; stir in cornstarch.
2. Heat oil in a wok over medium heat; add shrimp mixture.
3. Cook until light brown, about 5 minutes. Transfer to a plate.
4. Stir garlic into the wok; cook until fragrant, about 1 minute.
5. Add egg; cook and stir until scrambled, about 3 minutes.
6. Mix in mushrooms; cook and stir until softened, about 5 minutes.
7. Stir mixed vegetables into the wok; cook until softened, 3 to 5 minutes.
8. Mix in apple and raisins; add curry powder.
9. Cook and stir until fragrant, about 3 minutes.
10. Mix rice into the wok; season with soy sauce, salt, and pepper.
11. Cook and stir until rice is heated through, 3 to 5 minutes.
12. Add shrimp and green onion; cook and stir until warmed through, 2 to 4 minutes.

Shrimp and Black Bean Stir Fry

Ingredients:

1/2 medium-size red onion, sliced
1 medium-size red bell pepper, sliced
3 tbsps. olive oil, divided
1 cup corn kernels
1 lb. peeled and deveined large, raw shrimp
3 garlic cloves, sliced
1 cup chopped fresh mango or pineapple
1 (15-oz.) can black beans, drained and rinsed
1/2 cup teriyaki baste-and-glaze sauce
1/4 cup pineapple juice
Hot cooked rice
Garnish: cilantro leaves

Directions:

1. Prepare noodles according to package directions.
2. Drain.
3. Combine 3 tbsps. water and next 4 ingredients (through cornstarch) in a small bowl, stirring with a whisk. Set aside.
4. Combine red pepper, black pepper, and shrimp in a medium bowl; toss to coat.
5. Heat a wok over high heat.
6. Add 1 1/2 tsps. oil to pan; swirl to coat.
7. Add shrimp mixture; cook 3 minutes or until shrimp are almost done, turning once.
8. Remove shrimp mixture from pan.
9. Add remaining 1 1/2 tsps. oil to pan; swirl to coat.
10. Add onion, bell pepper, and ginger; cook 2 minutes, stirring occasionally. Return shrimp mixture and juice mixture to pan.
11. Add mango; cook 1 minute or until liquid thickens slightly and shrimp are done.
12. Sprinkle with basil. Serve over noodles.

Fried Brown Rice with Snow Peas and Peanuts

Ingredients:

1 tbsp. peanut oil
1/2 cup thinly sliced onion
1 tsp. minced garlic
1 1/2 cups sliced snow peas
1/4 cup peanuts
1 (8.8-oz.) pouch precooked brown rice
1 tbsp. rice vinegar
1 tbsp. lower-sodium soy sauce

Directions:

1. Heat a large wok over medium-high heat.
2. Add peanut oil; swirl.
3. Add onion and garlic; stir-fry 1 minute.
4. Add snow peas and peanuts; stir-fry 2 minutes.
5. Add rice; stir-fry 1 minute.
6. Stir in vinegar and soy sauce; stir-fry 1 minute.

Beef and Broccoli

Ingredients:

1 pound lean beef ,cut into thin strips
1 tbsp. soy sauce
1 tbsp. sherry
2 tbsps. oil for high-heat frying
1 small yellow onion ,halved and then sliced
1 tbsp. minced fresh garlic
1 tbsp. minced fresh ginger
4 cups uncooked broccoli florets, chopped
1 cup bean sprouts
For the Sauce:
1/3 cup soy sauce
1/3 cup water
1/3 cup brown sugar
1 tbsp. sherry
1 tbsp. toasted sesame seed oil
1/2 tsp. freshly ground black pepper
1 1/2 tbsps. cornstarch

Directions:

1. Toss the beef strips with the soy sauce and sherry. Set aside until ready to use.
2. Combine the sauce ingredients until the cornstarch is dissolved. Set aside until ready to use.
3. Heat the oil over high heat in a wok. Once very hot, add the beef and fry until lightly browned, about 2 minutes.
4. Add the onions, garlic and ginger and fry for another minute.
5. Add a little more oil if necessary.
6. Add the broccoli and fry for another minute or until crisp-tender.
7. Stir in the bean sprouts.
8. Stir in the sauce and simmer for another minute.
9. Serve immediately with steamed rice.

Sesame Beef Stir Fry

Beef Marinade Ingredients:

2 tsp minced garlic
1 Tbsp grated fresh ginger
2 Tbsp reduced sodium soy sauce
1 Tbsp rice vinegar
1 Tbsp sesame oil
1 Tbsp sesame seeds
1/2 tsp Chinese 5 spice
1/4 tsp black pepper

Stir Fry Ingredients:

1 lb flank steak, thinly sliced
1 cup snow peas, sliced in half across
1/2 cup sliced carrots
8 green onions, sliced
1/4 cup beef broth
2 Tbsp reduced sodium soy sauce
1-2 Tbsp honey or light brown sugar
1 Tbsp rice vinegar
1/2 Tbsp minced garlic
2 tsp sesame oil
1 tsp grated fresh ginger
1 tsp cornstarch
1/2 tsp red pepper flakes
2 Tbsp vegetable oil (for cooking)

Directions:

1. Combine marinade ingredients in bowl and add flank steak. Set aside 15 minutes.
2. Heat 1 tbsp vegetable oil in a wok over medium high heat. Remove excess marinade from steak and cook in a single layer, for 2-3 minutes, stirring to cook both sides. Depending on the size of your pan, you may need to do this in batches. Remove steak to plate.
3. Heat remaining 1 Tbsp vegetable oil, then add peas, carrots and green onion and cook stirring often, 2-3 minutes.
4. Whisk together broth, soy sauce, honey/brown sugar, rice vinegar, garlic, sesame oil, fresh ginger, cornstarch, and red pepper flakes. Add steak and sauce to wok, stirring to combine. Sauce will thicken.
5. Stir in cooked ramen noodles if using, and serve.

Pineapple Fried Rice

Ingredients:

1 cup uncooked white rice
2 cups water
2 tbsps. sesame oil
3 green onions, thinly sliced including tops
1 cup diced ham
1/2 cup peas
1 (8 oz.) can pineapple chunks, drained
1 egg, beaten
1 tbsp. white sugar
1 tsp. salt
1/2 tsp. white pepper
1/2 tsp. garlic powder
1/4 cup soy sauce

Directions:

1. Bring the rice and water to a boil in a saucepan over high heat.
2. Reduce heat to medium-low, cover, and simmer until the rice is tender, and the liquid has been absorbed, 20 to 25 minutes.
3. Spread cooked rice out on a rimmed baking sheet and refrigerate until cooled, about 20 minutes.
4. Heat sesame oil in a wok over medium-high heat.
5. Cook and stir the green onions, ham, and peas in the hot oil until onions have softened, about 2 minutes.
6. Stir the pineapple chunks into the wok; cook until pineapple begins to darken, about 2 minute. Push ingredients to the side of the wok, and pour beaten egg in the center.
7. Cook until egg begins to set, about 30 seconds.
8. Stir together all contents of the wok.
9. Mix the cooled rice, sugar, salt, white pepper, and garlic powder into the wok; stir constantly to keep from sticking.
10. Cook until heated through, about 3 minutes.
11. Sprinkle the rice with the soy sauce, and stir to combine.

Shrimp Fried Rice

Ingredients:

1 1/2 cups uncooked white rice
3 cups water
4 tbsps. vegetable oil
1 cup fresh bean sprouts
1/2 cup chopped onion
1 1/2 cups cooked medium shrimp, peeled, deveined without tail
1/4 cup chopped green onion
2 eggs, beaten
1 tsp. salt
1/4 tsp. ground black pepper
4 tbsps. soy sauce
1/4 tsp. sesame oil

Directions:

1. In a saucepan bring water to a boil.
2. Add rice and stir.
3. Reduce heat, cover and simmer for 20 minutes. Set aside and allow rice to cool.
4. Heat a wok for 2 minutes. When the wok is hot, pour in vegetable oil, bean sprouts and onions.
5. Mix well and cook for 3 minutes.
6. Mix in cooled rice and shrimp and cook for another 3 minutes.
7. Stirring constantly.
8. Mix in green onions, eggs, salt, pepper, soy sauce and sesame oil.
9. Cook for another 4 minutes, stirring continuously, until eggs are cooked and everything is blended evenly.

Cashew Chicken Stir Fry

Ingredients:

4 chicken breast halves, cut into bite-size pieces
1 tbsp. Cajun seasoning blend
1 1/4 cups chicken broth
1 tbsp. cornstarch
4 tsps. soy sauce, divided
2 tbsps. olive oil, divided
2 cups shredded cabbage
25 sugar snap peas, chopped
10 small spears fresh asparagus, chopped
3 stalks celery, chopped
1/2 red bell pepper, cut into thin strips
2 green onions, chopped
1 (8 oz.) can sliced bamboo shoots, drained
1/2 cup cashews
1 pinch paprika, or to taste

Directions:

1. Sprinkle chicken pieces with Cajun seasoning.
2. Whisk chicken broth, cornstarch, and 3 tsps. soy sauce together in a bowl until completely blended.
3. Heat 1 tbsp. olive oil in a deep frying pan or wok over high heat.
4. Cook and stir chicken in hot oil until cooked through, 6 to 10 minutes.
5. Remove chicken from pan and drain any accumulated liquids.
6. Heat remaining 1 tbsp. olive oil in the frying pan or wok over high heat.
7. Stir fry cabbage, snap peas, asparagus, celery, red bell pepper, green onions, and bamboo shoots for 1 minute.
8. Stir in 1 tsp. soy sauce. Continue cooking until vegetables are tender but still crisp, about 3 minutes.
9. Stir chicken into cabbage mixture.
10. Pour chicken broth mixture over chicken mixture, reduce heat to medium, and simmer until sauce thickens, about 1 minute.
11. Reduce heat to low; add cashews and cook until heated through, 1 minute.
12. Sprinkle with paprika.

Blueberry Chicken Stir Fry

Ingredients:

1 tbsp. chopped garlic
1/2 cup fresh blueberries
1/2 cup peach preserves
1 tbsp. sesame oil
3 tbsps. Dijon mustard
1/3 cup rice wine vinegar
3 tbsps. brown sugar
1 tbsp. soy sauce
1/4 cup olive oil
2 (4 oz.) chicken breast halves, cut into bite size pieces
1 cup sliced fresh mushrooms
1 tsp. minced fresh ginger
1 pinch garlic salt, or to taste
Ground black pepper to taste
2/3 cup chopped green onions
4 cups frozen mixed vegetables
4 cups cooked brown rice
1 tsp. toasted sesame seeds

Directions:

1. Place garlic, blueberries, peach preserves, sesame oil, mustard, vinegar, sugar, and soy sauce in a blender; cover and blend until smooth.
2. Heat oil in a wok over high heat; cook and stir chicken and mushrooms until chicken is no longer pink in the center and juices run clear, about 7 minutes.
3. Stir in ginger, garlic salt, and black pepper; cook and stir until fragrant, about 1 minute.
4. Toss green onions and mixed vegetables with chicken; pour blueberry sauce over vegetable mixture. Continue cooking on medium-high heat until sauce comes to a boil, about 10 minutes.
5. Reduce heat to low and cook until vegetables are tender, 2 to 4 minutes.
6. Remove from heat and allow sauce to cool for 3 minutes. Serve over brown rice and sprinkle with sesame seeds.

Grapes and Rice Stir Fry

Ingredients:

1 tbsp. vegetable oil
1 cup sliced red grapes
1 cup cubed cooked chicken
2 cups cooked rice
1/4 cup chicken broth

Directions:

1. Heat the vegetable oil in a wok over medium high heat.
2. Stir in the grapes and chicken; cook and stir until the chicken is hot, and the grapes are tender, about 3 minutes.
3. Add the rice and chicken broth; continue cooking until the rice is hot, about 2 minutes more.

Chicken and Broccoli Stir-fry

Ingredients:

1 pound chicken breast (about 2 breasts), cubed
3 scallions, whites only, thinly sliced on an angle
2 cloves garlic, minced
1 (1 inch) piece peeled fresh ginger, minced
1 tbsp. soy sauce
2 tbsps. sugar
1 tbsp., plus 1 tsp. cornstarch
1 1/4 tsps. salt
1 tbsp. dry sherry
1 tbsp. dark sesame oil
1/3 cup water
3 tbsps. vegetable oil
3 cups broccoli stalks, sliced
3 cups broccoli florets
3/4 to 1 tsp. red chili flakes, optional
1 tbsp. hoisin sauce

Directions:

1. In a medium bowl, toss the chicken with the scallion whites, about half the garlic and ginger, the soy sauce, sugar, 1 tsp. of the cornstarch, 1 tsp. of the salt, the sherry, and the sesame oil. Marinate at room temperature for 15 minutes.
2. Mix the remaining cornstarch with 1/3 cup water.
3. Heat a wok over high heat.
4. Add 1 tbsp. of the oil and heat.
5. Add the broccoli stems, and stir-fry for 30 seconds.
6. Add the florets and the remaining garlic, ginger, 2 tbsps. of water, and season with 1/4 tsp. salt, and pepper.
7. Stir-fry until the broccoli is bright green but still crisp, about 2 minutes. Transfer to a plate.
8. Get the wok good and hot again, and then heat 2 more tbsps. oil.
9. Add the chicken and chili flakes if using.
10. Stir-fry until the chicken loses its raw color and gets a little brown, about 3 minutes.
11. Add the hoisin sauce, return the broccoli to the pan and toss to heat through.
12. Stir in the reserved cornstarch mixture and bring to a boil to thicken.
13. Add more water if need to thin the sauce, if necessary. Taste and season with salt and pepper, if you like. Mound the stir-fry on a serving platter or divide among 4 plates and garnish with sesame seeds; serve with rice.

Broccoli and Tofu Stir Fry

Ingredients:

1 tbsp. peanut oil
4 cloves garlic, minced
1 red bell pepper, seeded and sliced into strips
2 crowns broccoli, cut into florets
1/3 cup chicken broth
3 tbsps. soy sauce
1 tbsp. dry sherry
2 tsps. cornstarch
8 oz. extra firm tofu, diced
2 tbsps. cashew pieces

Directions:

1. Heat peanut oil in a wok over high heat.
2. Stir in garlic and cook for a few seconds until it begins to brown.
3. Add the bell pepper and broccoli; cook until the pepper begins to brown and soften, about 5 minutes.
4. Stir together the chicken broth, soy sauce, sherry, and cornstarch until dissolved.
5. Pour the sauce into the wok and bring to a boil.
6. Stir in the tofu, and cook until hot, about 1 minute. Garnish with cashew pieces to serve.

Stir-Fried Mushrooms with Baby Corn

Ingredients:

2 tbsps. cooking oil
3 cloves garlic, minced
1 onion, diced
8 baby corn ears, sliced
2/3 pound fresh mushrooms, sliced
1 tbsp. fish sauce
1 tbsp. light soy sauce
1 tbsp. oyster sauce
2 tsps. cornstarch
3 tbsps. water
1 red chile pepper, sliced
1/4 cup chopped fresh cilantro

Directions:

1. Heat the oil in a wok over medium heat; cook the garlic in the hot oil until browned, 5 to 7 minutes.
2. Add the onion and baby corn and cook until the onion is translucent, 5 to 7 minutes.
3. Add the mushrooms to the mixture and cook until slightly softened, about 2 minutes.
4. Pour the fish sauce, soy sauce, and oyster sauce into the mixture and stir until incorporated.
5. Whisk the cornstarch and water together in a small bowl until the cornstarch is dissolved into the water; pour into the mushroom mixture.
6. Cook and stir until thickened and glistening. Transfer to a serving dish; garnish with the chile pepper and cilantro to serve.

Baby Bok Choy with Garlic

Ingredients:

1 1/2 tbsps. rapeseed oil
2 tsps. minced garlic
1 pound baby bok choy
1 tbsp. soy sauce
1/2 tsp. white sugar
Salt and freshly ground black pepper
1/4 cup water
1/2 tsp. sesame oil (optional)

Directions:

1. Heat a wok over medium heat.
2. Add oil and allow to get hot.
3. Add garlic and stir-fry until fragrant, about 30 seconds.
4. Add bok choy and cook for 30 seconds.
5. Season with soy sauce, sugar, and salt and stir-fry for 1 minute.
6. Pour water into the wok, cover, and simmer until leaves are dark green and stems are tender, but still firm, 2 to 3 minutes.
7. Remove from heat, drizzle with sesame oil, and season with pepper.

Stir Fried Wok Vegetables

Ingredients:

2 tbsps. vegetable oil
1 tbsp. minced fresh ginger (optional)
3 serrano chile peppers, seeded and chopped (optional)
1/2 cup baby corn, cut in half
1 red bell pepper, seeded and cut into strips
2 pounds bok choy, stalks halved and cut into 1/4-inch sticks
3 cups fresh bean sprouts
1/4 cup Asian fish sauce (nuoc mam or nam pla)
3 tbsps. Chinese oyster sauce
4 green onions, thinly sliced
2 tbsps. chopped cilantro leaves (optional)
2 tbsps. toasted sesame seeds (optional)

Directions:

1. Heat vegetable oil in a wok over high heat. When the oil is hot, stir in ginger and minced chiles; cook and stir until the ginger is fragrant, about 30 seconds.
2. Add baby corn, red pepper, and bok choy stalks; stir fry until the red pepper has begun to soften, about 3 minutes.
3. Stir in bok choy leaves and bean sprouts; cook until the leaves have darkened and wilted, 1 to 2 minutes.
4. Pour in fish sauce and oyster sauce; sprinkle with green onions, and stir together. Serve sprinkled with chopped cilantro and toasted sesame seeds.

Stir Fried Sesame Vegetables with Rice

Ingredients:

1 1/2 cups vegetable broth
3/4 cup uncooked long-grain white rice
1 tbsp. margarine
1 tbsp. sesame seeds
2 tbsps. peanut oil
1/2 pound fresh asparagus, cut into pieces
1 large red bell pepper, cut into 1 inch pieces
1 large yellow onion, sliced
2 cups sliced mushrooms
2 tsps. minced fresh ginger root
1 tsp. minced garlic
3 tbsps. soy sauce
1 tbsp. sesame oil

Directions:

1. Preheat oven to 350 degrees F (175 degrees C).
2. In a saucepan combine broth, rice and margarine.
3. Cover and bring to a boil over high heat.
4. Reduce heat to low and simmer for 15 minutes, or until all liquid is absorbed.
5. Place sesame seeds on a small baking sheet and bake in preheated oven for 5 to 6 minutes, or until golden brown; set aside.
6. Meanwhile, heat peanut oil in a wok over medium-high heat until very hot.
7. Add asparagus, bell pepper, onion, mushrooms, ginger and garlic and stir-fry for 4 to 5 minutes, or until vegetables are tender but crisp.
8. Stir in soy-sauce and cook for 30 seconds.
9. Remove from heat and stir in sesame oil and toasted sesame seeds. Serve over rice.

Stir Fried Snow Peas and Mushrooms

Ingredients:

1 tbsp. sesame seeds
1 tbsp. olive oil
1/2 pound snow peas
4 oz. fresh mushrooms, thinly sliced
2 tbsps. teriyaki sauce

Directions:

1. In a medium wok over medium heat, cook the sesame seeds about 5 minutes, stirring frequently, until lightly browned.
2. Remove from heat, and set aside.
3. Heat oil in the wok over medium high heat.
4. Stir in snow peas and mushrooms, and cook 3 to 4 minutes, until tender.
5. Transfer snow peas and mushrooms to a medium bowl.
6. Toss with sesame seeds and teriyaki sauce, and serve warm.

Fried Rice with Chinese Sausage

Ingredients:

1/4 cup canola oil, divided
2 eggs, lightly beaten
1 tbsp. chopped ginger
1 tbsp. chopped garlic
1 carrot, finely diced
2 stalks celery, finely diced
3 links Chinese sausage, sliced
1 small bunch scallions, sliced, divided
4 cups cooked white rice
1/4 cup low-sodium soy sauce
1 tbsp. rice wine vinegar

Directions:

1. Heat 2 tbsps. of canola oil in a wok over high heat.
2. Add the beaten eggs and fry until they are fully cooked. Transfer them to plate.
3. Add the remaining oil, ginger, garlic, carrot, and celery, and stir-fry for 2 minutes.
4. Add the sausage and half of the scallions and cook for 1 minute.
5. Add the cooked rice, soy sauce and rice wine vinegar.
6. Stir-fry until the rice is hot, about 2 minutes.
7. Stir in the reserved eggs and transfer to a serving dish. Garnish with the remaining scallions and serve.

Fried Brown Rice with Shrimp and Snap Peas

Ingredients:

1 1/2 (8.8-oz.) pouches precooked brown rice
2 tbsps. soy sauce
1 tbsp. sambal oelek (ground fresh chile paste)
1 tbsp. honey
2 tbsps. peanut oil, divided
10 oz. medium shrimp, peeled and deveined
3 large eggs, lightly beaten
1 1/2 cups sugar snap peas, diagonally sliced
1/3 cup unsalted, dry-roasted peanuts
1/8 tsp. salt
3 garlic cloves, crushed

Directions:

1. Heat rice according to package directions.
2. Combine soy sauce, sambal oelek, and honey in a large bowl.
3. Combine 1 tsp. peanut oil and shrimp in a medium bowl; toss to coat. Heat a wok over high heat.
4. Add shrimp to pan, and stir-fry 2 minutes.
5. Add shrimp to soy sauce mixture; toss to coat shrimp.
6. Add 1 tsp. peanut oil to pan; swirl to coat.
7. Add eggs to pan; cook 45 seconds or until set.
8. Remove eggs from pan; cut into bite-sized pieces.
9. Add 1 tbsp. oil to pan; swirl to coat.
10. Add rice; stir-fry 4 minutes.
11. Add rice to shrimp mixture.
12. Add remaining 1 tsp. oil to pan; swirl to coat.
13. Add sugar snap peas, peanuts, salt, and garlic to pan; stir-fry for 2 minutes or until peanuts begin to brown.
14. Add shrimp mixture and egg to pan, and cook for 2 minutes or until thoroughly heated.
15. Add 1 tbsp. oil to pan; swirl to coat.
16. Add rice; stir-fry 4 minutes.
17. Add rice to shrimp mixture.
18. Add remaining 1 tsp. oil to pan; swirl to coat.
19. Add sugar snap peas, peanuts, salt, and garlic to pan; stir-fry for 2 minutes or until peanuts begin to brown.
20. Add shrimp mixture and egg to pan, and cook for 2 minutes or until thoroughly heated.

Vietnamese Caramel Pork

Ingredients:

1 tbsp. dark sesame oil
1 (1-lb.) pork tenderloin, trimmed and cut into 1-inch pieces
1 cup chopped onion
1 cup chopped carrot
1 tbsp. minced peeled fresh ginger
5 garlic cloves, thinly sliced
1 cup unsalted chicken stock
3 tbsps. dark brown sugar
1 tbsp. fish sauce
1 tbsp. lower-sodium soy sauce
2 tsps. cornstarch
2 tsps. cornstarch
2 tsps. rice vinegar
1/2 tsp. crushed red pepper
1 (8.8-oz.) package precooked white rice
1 cup thinly sliced napa (Chinese) cabbage
1/4 cup chopped unsalted roasted peanuts
1/4 cup cilantro leaves
4 lime wedges

Directions:

1. Heat a wok over high heat.
2. Add oil to pan; swirl to coat.
3. Add pork; stir-fry 6 minutes, browning on all sides.
4. Remove pork from pan.
5. Add onion, carrot, ginger, and garlic to pan; stir-fry 2 minutes.
6. Combine stock and next 6 ingredients (through red pepper) in a bowl, stirring with a whisk.
7. Add stock mixture to pan; bring to a boil.
8. Reduce heat; simmer 4 minutes or until sauce is thick and bubbly. Return pork to pan; cook 1 minute, stirring to coat.
9. Spoon 1/2 cup rice onto each of 4 plates; top each serving with 3/4 cup pork mixture and 1/4 cup cabbage.
10. Sprinkle each serving with 1 tbsp. peanuts and 1 tbsp. cilantro. Serve with lime wedges.

Fiery Pepper Chicken

Ingredients:

1 tsp. Chinese cooking wine
1/2 tsp. salt
1/2 lb. boneless chicken, cut into
1/2 inch cubes
1/4 cup cornstarch, or as needed
3 cups peanut oil for frying
4 cloves garlic, minced
1 tbsp. minced fresh ginger root
2 green onions, julienned
2 long, green chilies - cut into 1/2-inch pieces
2 cups dried chilies, chopped
2 tbsps. Szechuan peppercorns
2 tsps. soy sauce
2 tsps. Chinese cooking wine
1/2 tsp. white sugar
1/2 tsp. salt

Directions:

1. Stir together 1 tsp. cooking wine and 1/2 tsp. salt in a bowl; add the chicken and stir to coat. Allow to marinate 2 to 3 minutes.
2. Place the marinated chicken in a large, sealable plastic bag with the cornstarch and shake to coat.
3. Heat the peanut oil in a wok over high heat. Fry the chicken in the oil until it begins to crisp around the edges, 7 to 10 minutes.
4. Remove the chicken to a paper towel-lined plate to drain. Reserve 2 tbsps. of the oil, discarding the rest.
5. Reheat the reserved oil in the wok over medium-high heat; cook and stir the garlic, ginger, and green onions in the oil until fragrant, about 1 minute.
6. Add the green chilies, crushed dried chilies, and Szechuan peppercorns; continue frying about 20 seconds more. Return the chicken to the wok; stir in the soy sauce, 2 tsps. cooking wine, sugar, and 1/2 tsp. salt until thoroughly combined.
7. Remove from heat and serve immediately.

Shrimp and Cabbage Stir-Fry

Ingredients:

1 large egg white
1 tbsp. plus 2 tsps. cornstarch
1 tbsp. plus 1 tsp. soy sauce
1 1/4 pounds medium shrimp, peeled and deveined
2 tsps. hoisin sauce
1 1/2 tsps. sherry vinegar or rice wine vinegar
1/2 cup low-sodium chicken broth or water
2 tbsps. vegetable oil
4 scallions, cut into 1/2-inch pieces, white and green parts separated
1 tbsp. finely grated peeled ginger
1 clove garlic, finely grated
1 pound Napa cabbage (1/2 head), cut into 1-inch pieces
Cooked white rice, for serving (optional)

Directions:

1. Whisk the egg white, 1 tbsp. cornstarch and 1 tsp. soy sauce in a large bowl until frothy.
2. Add the shrimp and toss to coat. Refrigerate 10 minutes.
3. Meanwhile, whisk the hoisin sauce, vinegar and the remaining 1 tbsp. soy sauce and 2 tsps. cornstarch in a small bowl, then whisk in the chicken broth. Set aside.
4. Drain the shrimp. Heat the vegetable oil in a wok over medium-high heat, then stir-fry the scallion whites, ginger and garlic, about 30 seconds.
5. Add the shrimp and stir-fry until almost cooked through, about 3 minutes.
6. Add the cabbage and stir-fry until wilted and the shrimp are just cooked through, about 2 more minutes.
7. Stir the hoisin sauce mixture, then add to the wok and simmer, stirring occasionally, 2 minutes.
8. Stir in the scallion greens. Serve with rice, if desired.

Tsao Mi Fun (Taiwanese Fried Rice Noodles)

Ingredients:

1/2 lb. thinly sliced pork loin
1/4 cup soy sauce
1/4 cup rice wine
1 tsp. white pepper
1 tsp. Chinese five-spice powder
1 tsp. cornstarch
4 dried Chinese black mushrooms
1 (8 oz.) package dried rice vermicelli
1/4 cup vegetable oil, divided
2 eggs, beaten
1/4 clove garlic, minced
1 tbsp. dried small shrimp
3 carrots, cut into matchstick strips
1/2 onion, chopped
3 cups bean sprouts
4 leaves napa cabbage, thinly slicedsalt to taste
3 sprigs fresh cilantro for garnish

Directions:

1. Place the pork into a mixing bowl and pour in the soy sauce and rice wine.
2. Sprinkle with the white pepper, five-spice powder, and cornstarch.
3. Mix well, then set aside to marinate. Soak the mushrooms in a bowl of cold water for 20 minutes, then pour off the water, cut off and discard the stems of the mushrooms.
4. Slice the mushrooms thinly and reserve.
5. Soak the rice vermicelli in a separate bowl of cold water for 10 minutes, then pour off the water and set the noodles aside.
6. Heat 1 tbsp. of the vegetable oil in a wok over medium heat.
7. Pour in the eggs, and cook until firm, flipping once, to make a pancake.
8. Remove the egg pancake, and allow to cool, then thinly slice and place into a large bowl. Heat 2 more tbsps. of the vegetable oil in the wok over high heat.
9. Stir in the garlic and dried shrimp, and cook until the shrimp become aromatic, about 20 seconds. Next, add the pork along with the marinade, and cook until the pork is no longer pink, about 4 minutes.
10. Stir in the carrots and onion, and cook until the carrots begin to soften, about 3 minutes.
11. Finally, add the bean sprouts, napa cabbage, and sliced mushrooms; cook and stir until the vegetables are tender, about 3 minutes more.
12. Scrape the pork mixture into the bowl along with the eggs, then wipe out the wok and return it to the stove over medium-high heat.

13. Heat the remaining vegetable oil in the wok, then stir in the drained rice vermicelli noodles.
14. Cook and stir for a few minutes until the noodles soften, then stir in the reserved pork mixture. Scrape the mixture in to a serving bowl and garnish with cilantro to serve.

Pad Thai Noodles

Ingredients:

2/3 cup dried rice vermicelli
1/4 cup peanut oil2/3 cup thinly sliced firm tofu
1 large egg, beaten4 cloves garlic, finely chopped
1/4 cup vegetable broth
2 tbsps. fresh lime juice
2 tbsps. soy sauce
1 tbsp. white sugar
1 tsp. salt
1/2 tsp. dried red chili flakes
3 tbsps. chopped peanuts
1 lb. bean sprouts, divided
3 green onions, whites thinly sliced and greens sliced into thin lengths, divided
3 tbsps. chopped peanuts
2 limes, cut into wedges for garnish

Directions:

1. Soak rice vermicelli noodles in a bowl filled with hot water until softened, 30 minutes to 1 hour.
2. Drain and set aside.
3. Heat peanut oil over medium heat in a large wok.
4. Cook and stir tofu in the wok, turning the pieces until they are golden on all sides.
5. Remove tofu with a slotted spoon and drain on plate lined with paper towels.
6. Pour all but 1 tbsp. of used oil from the wok into a small bowl; it will be used again in a later step.
7. Heat the remaining 1 tbsp. of oil in the wok over medium heat until it starts to sizzle.
8. Pour in beaten egg and lightly toss in the hot oil to scramble the egg.
9. Remove egg from the wok and set aside.
10. Pour reserved peanut oil in the small bowl back into the wok.
11. Toss garlic and drained noodles in wok until they are coated with oil.
12. Stir in vegetable broth, lime juice, soy sauce, and sugar.
13. Toss and gently push noodles around the pan to coat with sauce.
14. Gently mix in tofu, scrambled egg, salt, chili flakes, and 3 tbsps. peanuts; toss to mix all ingredients.
15. Mix in bean sprouts and green onions, reserving about 1 tbsp. of each for garnish.
16. Cook and stir until bean sprouts have softened slightly, 1 to 2 minutes.
17. Arrange noodles on a warm serving platter and garnish with 3 tbsps. peanuts and reserved bean sprouts and green onions.
18. Place lime wedges around the edges of the platter.

Thai Fried Rice with Pineapple and Chicken

Ingredients:

3 slices bacon, diced
3 shallots, sliced
4 oz. chicken breast, cut into small cubes
4 tsps. curry powder, divided
3 egg yolks, beaten
1 tsp. vegetable oil, or as needed
3 cups cooked jasmine rice
1 red Thai bird chile pepper, finely chopped
2 tbsps. whole cilantro leaves
1 tbsp. soy sauce
2 tsps. fish sauce
1/2 tsp. white sugar
4 oz. tiger prawns, peeled and deveined
1/4 cup chopped fresh pineapple
3 green onions, finely chopped

Directions:

1. Place bacon in a wok.
2. Cook and stir over medium-high heat until crisp, about 10 minutes.
3. Remove bacon with a slotted spoon and reserve bacon drippings in the wok.
4. Cook and stir shallots in bacon drippings over medium-high heat until fragrant and light brown, 1 to 2 minutes.
5. Stir chicken into shallots and cook without stirring until browned on one side, 45 seconds to 1 minute; stir. Continue cooking until chicken is browned, about 1 minute.
6. Add 2 tsps. curry powder; stir until chicken is coated.
7. Make a well in the center of chicken and pour oil into center of the well; add egg yolks.
8. Cook and stir egg yolks until set, 1 to 2 minutes.
9. Add rice and stir, breaking up rice.
10. Mix chile pepper, cilantro, soy sauce, remaining 2 tsps. curry powder, fish sauce, and sugar into rice mixture; add shrimp and cook until shrimp is cooked through and pink, about 2 minutes. Fold pineapple, green onions, and bacon into rice mixture.

Pork Tofu with Watercress and Bean Sprouts

Ingredients:

1 (2 lb.) boneless pork loin, cut into 1/2 inch strips
1 cup soy sauce
3/4 cup water
1 tsp. minced fresh ginger root
1 tbsp. coarsely ground black pepper
2 bunches watercress, rinsed, dried, cut into 1/2 inch lengths
8 oz. bean sprouts
1 (16 oz.) package firm tofu, drained and cubed

Directions:

1. Place pork in a wok over medium heat.
2. Cook and stir until pork is browned on all sides, about 5 minutes.
3. Stir in the soy sauce, water, ginger, and black pepper; bring to a boil over medium-high heat.
4. Reduce heat to medium, cover, and simmer until meat is tender, about 40 minutes.
5. Stir in the watercress and bean sprouts, and continue to simmer until tender yet still crisp, about 10 minutes more.
6. Mix in the tofu, cover, and simmer 5 minutes more.

Chinese Braised Zucchini

Ingredients:

2 tbsps. sesame oil
1 small yellow onion, diced
3 cloves garlic, minced
1 tbsp. Chinese black bean sauce
2 Thai chile peppers, seeded and chopped
4 zucchinis, cut into
1/2-inch slices
1 tbsp. minced fresh ginger root
1 tbsp. soy sauce
1/4 cup water

Directions:

1. Heat the sesame oil in a wok over medium-high heat.
2. Stir fry the onion and garlic in the hot oil until the onion begins to soften, about 2 minutes.
3. Stir in the black bean sauce and chile peppers, and continue stir frying about 30 seconds to coat the onions with the black bean sauce.
4. Stir in the zucchini, ginger, soy sauce, and water.
5. Cover, reduce the heat to medium-low, and cook for 15 minutes until the zucchini is soft, stirring occasionally.

Caramelized Pork Belly (Thit Kho)

Ingredients:

2 lbs. pork belly, trimmed
2 tbsps. white sugar
5 shallots, sliced
3 cloves garlic, chopped
3 tbsps. fish sauce
Ground black pepper to taste
13 fluid oz. coconut water
6 hard-boiled eggs, peeled

Directions:

1. Slice pork belly into 1-inch pieces layered with skin, fat, and meat.
2. Heat sugar in a large wok or pot over medium heat until it melts and caramelizes into a light brown syrup, about 5 minutes.
3. Add pork and increase heat to high.
4. Cook and stir to render some of the pork fat, 3 to 5 minutes.
5. Stir shallots and garlic into the wok.
6. Add fish sauce and black pepper; stir to evenly coat pork.
7. Pour in coconut water and bring to a boil.
8. Add eggs, reduce heat to low, and simmer, covered, until pork is tender, about 1 hour.
9. Remove wok from the heat and let stand, about 10 minutes. Skim the fat from the surface of the dish.

Chicken, Snow Pea, and Cashew Fried Rice

Ingredients:

1 lb. skinless, boneless chicken breasts, cut into thin strips
1/4 cup teriyaki sauce, divided
3 tbsps. vegetable oil, divided
3 scallions, thinly sliced
2 cloves garlic, minced
1 tbsp. minced fresh ginger root
8 oz. snow peas, trimmed
1/4 cup low-sodium chicken broth
4 cups cooked white rice
3 tbsps. chopped roasted cashews

Directions:

1. Combine chicken and 2 tbsps. teriyaki sauce in a bowl. Heat 1 1/2 tbsps. vegetable oil in a wok over high heat.
2. Add chicken; cook and stir until no longer pink in the center, 3 to 5 minutes. Transfer to a separate bowl.
3. Stir scallions, garlic, ginger, and remaining vegetable oil into wok until fragrant, about 1 minute.
4. Stir in snow peas and chicken broth; cover and cook until tender; 2 to 3 minutes.
5. Stir rice, cooked chicken, and remaining teriyaki sauce into wok; cook and stir until rice is heated through, 2 to 3 minutes.
6. Sprinkle with cashews.

Bitter Melon and Black Bean Sauce Beef

Ingredients:

Ice cubes
1 bitter melon, seeded and sliced
2 tsps. soy sauce, divided
2 tsps. cornstarch, divided
1/4 tsp. baking soda
6 oz. beef, sliced
1 tbsp. oil
1 tsp. oil
1/2 onion, sliced
2 cloves garlic
1 tbsp. chopped fresh ginger
1 tbsp. black bean sauce
1 tbsp. oyster sauce
1 pinch white sugar, or to taste
3/4 cup water
1 tsp. water
Salt to taste

Directions:

1. Fill a bowl with ice; add enough salted water to make an ice bath.
2. Bring a large pot of lightly salted water to a boil.
3. Cook the bitter melon in the boiling water until tender yet firm, about 2 minutes; strain the melon.
4. Place the melon into the ice bath; allow to sit until bitterness is extracted, about 1 hour.
5. Drain melon.
6. Whisk 1 tsp. soy sauce, 1 tsp. cornstarch, and baking soda together in a bowl.
7. Add beef and toss to evenly coat. Marinate in the refrigerator for 1 hour.
8. Heat wok on high until smoking.
9. Add 1 tbsp. oil. Lay beef evenly across the bottom of the wok; cook until browned, about 2 minutes per side.
10. Remove beef.
11. Pour in 1 tsp. of oil; allow to heat.
12. Add onion, garlic, and ginger; cook and stir until fragrant, about 30 seconds.
13. Stir in bitter melon; cook until combined, about 1 minute.
14. Stir black bean sauce into melon mixture.
15. Stir in remaining soy sauce, oyster sauce, and sugar.
16. Pour in 3/4 cup water; cover and let simmer until flavors combine, 2 to 3 minutes. Uncover and mix in remaining cornstarch and 1 tsp. water and stir until thickened.

Okra Stir Fry

Ingredients:

2 tbsps. vegetable oil
1 lb. small okra
1/2 tsp. ground turmeric
1 clove garlic, chopped
1/2 tsp. chopped fresh ginger
2 onions, cut into quarters
2 roma (plum) tomatoes, cut into quarters
1 tbsp. chopped fresh cilantro

Directions:

1. Heat vegetable oil in a wok over medium-high heat; cook and stir okra until tender and golden brown, about 3 minutes. Transfer okra to a plate.
2. Sprinkle turmeric into hot oil; heat until turmeric becomes aromatic, 1 to 2 minutes.
3. Add garlic, ginger, onions, and tomatoes; cook and stir until onions are tender, about 10 minutes.
4. Stir okra into onion mixture. Garnish with cilantro.

Jasmine Rice with Bok Choy

Ingredients:

1 tbsp. butter
1 head bok choy, chopped
2 cups chicken stock
1 cup uncooked jasmine rice
1 tbsp. olive oil
1 tbsp. chopped fresh chives, or to taste
1 pinch ground black pepper

Directions:

1. Melt butter in a deep wok or wide pot over medium heat.
2. Add bok choy and stir-fry until soft, about 5 minutes.
3. Add chicken stock and increase heat to high.
4. Bring to a boil.
5. Add rice, olive oil, and chives and stir well.
6. Cover with a tight-fitting lid, reduce heat to a simmer, and cook for 20 minutes. Check rice after 10 minutes to make sure it is pacing well; overcooking will turn the rice dry, undercooking will produce hard rice.
7. Season with pepper and serve.

Bok Choy with Pine Nuts and Sesame Seeds

Ingredients:

1 tsp. sesame oil
1 red onion, finely sliced
2 cloves garlic, finely sliced
1 lb. baby bok choy, trimmed
1 tbsp. light soy sauce
2 tsps. fish sauce
1 tbsp. toasted pine nuts
2 tsps. toasted sesame seeds
1 cup Thai basil (optional)

Directions:

1. Heat sesame oil in a wok over low heat.
2. Cook and stir onion and garlic until soft, about 5 minutes.
3. Add bok choy and continue to stir-fry.
4. Add soy sauce, fish sauce, pine nuts, toasted sesame seeds and Thai basil.
5. Stir-fry until the green tips of the bok choy and the basil are just wilted, about 3 minutes.

Baby Bok Choy and Shiitake Stir-Fry

Ingredients:

1/2 cup chicken or mushroom broth
2 tbsps. oyster sauce
2 tbsps. rice wine or dry sherry
2 tsps. cornstarch
1 1/2 tbsps. peanut or vegetable oil
2 medium garlic cloves, minced
1 (1 1/2 inch) piece ginger root, peeled and minced
1/2 tsp. kosher salt
3 1/2 oz. shiitake mushrooms, stems discarded and caps sliced
1 1/4 lbs. baby bok choy, chopped

Directions:

1. Stir together broth, oyster sauce, rice wine, and cornstarch in a small bowl.
2. Heat oil in a wok over medium-high heat until it shimmers.
3. Stir-fry garlic and ginger with salt until fragrant, about 30 seconds.
4. Add shiitakes and stir-fry until softened, 1 to 2 minutes.
5. Add bok choy and stir-fry until crisp-tender, 2 to 3 minutes.
6. Re-stir cornstarch mixture.
7. Make a well in vegetables and add cornstarch mixture.
8. Bring to a boil and toss to coat vegetables. Serve immediately.

Lemongrass Chicken

Ingredients:

1 1/2 lbs. chicken thighs, cut into thin strips
3 tbsps. fish sauce
1 1/2 tbsps. honey
2 tbsps. vegetable oil
1 1/2 red bell peppers, cut into strips
1/4 cup chopped lemongrass
1/4 cup grated fresh ginger root
4 cloves garlic, chopped
1/3 cup chopped green onions
1/4 cup chicken broth
1 tbsp. white sugar
1/2 tsp. red pepper flakes
Salt and ground black pepper to taste

Directions:

1. Mix chicken, fish sauce, and honey together in a bowl; cover with plastic wrap and refrigerate for at least 30 minutes.
2. Heat a wok over medium-high heat; swirl in oil.
3. Add red bell peppers, lemongrass, ginger, and garlic; cook until red bell pepper strips tender, about 5 minutes.
4. Add chicken mixture; saute until chicken is no longer pink and the juices run clear, about 5 minutes.
5. Stir green onions, chicken broth, sugar, red pepper flakes, salt, and pepper into the wok. Simmer, uncovered, until sauce thickens, about 5 minutes.

Panang Curry with Chicken

Ingredients:

5 tbsps. Panang curry paste cooking oil
4 cups coconut milk
2/3 lb. skinless, boneless chicken breast, cubed
2 tbsps. palm sugar
2 tbsps. fish sauce, or to taste
6 kaffir lime leaves, torn
2 fresh red chile peppers, sliced
1/4 cup fresh Thai basil leaves

Directions:

1. Fry the curry paste in the oil in a wok over medium heat until fragrant.
2. Stir the coconut milk into the curry paste and bring to a boil.
3. Add the chicken; cook and stir until the chicken is nearly cooked through, 10 to 15 minutes.
4. Stir the palm sugar, fish sauce, and lime leaves into the mixture; simmer together for 5 minutes. Taste and adjust the saltiness by adding more fish sauce if necessary. Garnish with sliced red chile peppers and Thai basil leaves to serve.

Shrimp and Fruit Fried Rice

Ingredients:

1 tbsp. vegetable oil, divided
2 eggs, beaten
1/2 lb. peeled and deveined medium shrimp
1 (1 inch) piece fresh ginger root, minced
2 red onions, sliced
3 green chile peppers, chopped
2/3 cup fresh pineapple, diced
1/2 cup orange segments
6 walnuts, chopped
2 cups cold, cooked white rice
1 tbsp. soy sauce
2 tbsps. chopped fresh cilantro
Salt and pepper to taste

Directions:

1. Heat 1 tsp. of the vegetable oil in a wok over medium-high heat.
2. Pour in the onions, and cook until just set; set aside. Increase the heat to high, and pour another 1 tsp. of oil to the wok.
3. Stir in the shrimp, and cook until the shrimp turn pink, and are no longer translucent in the center, about 3 minutes; set aside.
4. Wipe out the wok, and heat the remaining tsp. of oil over high heat.
5. Stir in the ginger, and cook quickly for a few seconds until the ginger begins to turn golden brown.
6. Stir in the onion and chile peppers; cook for a minute or two until the onions begin to soften and turn brown around the edges.
7. Add the pineapple and oranges, and gently cook until the pineapple is hot.
8. Stir in the rice, walnuts, and soy sauce.
9. Stir for a few minutes until the rice is hot. Fold in the egg, shrimp, and cilantro.
10. Season to taste with salt and pepper, and cook to reheat.

Spicy Ma Po Tofu

Ingredients:

1 (16 oz.) package soft tofu, cut into 1/3-inch cubes
1 tbsp. cornstarch
1 tbsp. water, or as needed
6 1/2 tbsps. vegetable oil
2 spring onions, roughly chopped
1 (3/4 inch thick) slice fresh ginger, chopped
2 tsps. Sichuan peppercorns
1 clove garlic, minced
5 oz. ground pork
1 tbsp. doubanjiang (spicy broad bean paste)
2 tsps. rice wine
1 tsp. soy sauce
1 tsp. salt, or to taste

Directions:

1. Place tofu in a bowl and cover with boiling water. Let sit for 1 minute; drain.
2. Mix water and cornstarch together in a bowl to make a runny paste.
3. Heat oil in a wok over medium heat.
4. Cook and stir spring onions, ginger, peppercorns, and garlic until fragrant, about 1 minute.
5. Stir in ground pork, doubanjiang paste, rice wine, and soy sauce; cook, stirring frequently, until pork is browned, about 5 minutes.
6. Stir drained tofu into the wok.
7. Cook and stir until coated with sauce, about 2 minutes.
8. Season with salt.
9. Pour in cornstarch paste and mix well until sauce thickens, about 1 minute.

Vegan Red Curry Tofu and Vegetables

Ingredients:

1 (12 oz.) package firm tofu, cubed
3 tbsps. light soy sauce
1 (14 oz.) can coconut milk
1 tbsp. Thai red curry paste
8 oz. broccoli florets
1 (4 oz.) package sliced fresh mushrooms
1 leek, cut lengthwise, washed, trimmed, and sliced thin
1 carrot, cut into matchsticks
1 squeeze lemon juice
1 pinch white sugar

Directions:

1. Combine tofu and 3 tbsps. soy sauce in a small bowl and marinate for about 20 minutes.
2. Remove the solid top layer of coconut cream from the coconut milk can and heat in a wok over medium heat.
3. Add curry paste and stir-fry for 2 minutes.
4. Add tofu, broccoli, mushrooms, leek, and carrot and stir-fry for 2 minutes.
5. Pour in remaining coconut milk and simmer until vegetables are soft, about 5 minutes.
6. Season with soy sauce, lemon juice, and sugar.

Coconut Curry Stir Fry

Ingredients:

1 1/2 cups coconut milk
1 tbsp. minced ginger
1 tbsp. lime juice
1 tbsp. fish sauce
1 tsp. oyster sauce
2 tsps. minced garlic
1/2 tsp. chile-garlic sauce (such as Sriracha)
2 tbsps. white sugar or sugar substitute
1 tbsp. avocado oil
1 lb. chicken breast, cut into bite-sized pieces
1/2 onion, sliced
1 1/2 tsps. curry powder
2 cups broccoli florets

Directions:

1. Mix coconut milk, ginger, lime juice, fish sauce, oyster sauce, garlic, chile-garlic sauce, and sugar together in a small bowl.
2. Heat avocado oil in a wok over medium-high heat.
3. Stir-fry chicken in the hot oil until no longer pink, 8 to 10 minutes.
4. Remove from wok and keep warm. Leave remaining avocado oil in wok.
5. Stir onion and curry powder into hot oil in wok; cook 2 minutes.
6. Stir in broccoli; stir-fry 3 minutes.
7. Add coconut milk mixture and bring to a boil.
8. Reduce heat to medium and simmer sauce and vegetables for 3 minutes. Return chicken to wok; cover and cook until chicken has heated through and vegetables are tender, about 3 minutes.

Crispy Ginger Beef

Ingredients:

3/4 cup cornstarch
1/2 cup water
2 eggs
1 lb. flank steak, cut into thin strips
1/2 cup canola oil, or as needed
1 large carrot, cut into matchstick-size pieces
1 green bell pepper, cut into matchstick-size pieces
1 red bell pepper, cut into matchstick-size pieces
3 green onions, chopped
1/4 cup minced fresh ginger root
5 garlic cloves, minced
1/2 cup white sugar
1/4 cup rice vinegar
3 tbsps. soy sauce
1 tbsp. sesame oil
1 tbsp. red pepper flakes, or to taste

Directions:

1. Place cornstarch in a large bowl; gradually whisk in water until smooth. Whisk eggs into cornstarch mixture; toss steak strips in mixture to coat.
2. Pour canola oil into wok 1-inch deep; heat oil over high heat until hot but not smoking.
3. Place 1/4 of the beef strips into hot oil; separate strips with a fork.
4. Cook, stirring frequently, until coating is crisp and golden, about 3 minutes.
5. Remove beef to drain on paper towels; repeat with remaining beef.
6. Drain off all but 1 tbsp. oil; cook and stir carrot, green bell pepper, red bell pepper, green onions, ginger, and garlic over high heat until lightly browned but still crisp, about 3 minutes.
7. Whisk sugar, rice vinegar, soy sauce, sesame oil, and red pepper together in a small bowl.
8. Pour sauce mixture over vegetables in wok; bring mixture to a boil.
9. Stir beef back into vegetable mixture; cook and stir just until heated through, about 3 minutes.

Yellow Squash and Tofu Stir Fry

Ingredients:

1 tbsp. olive oil, or as needed
3 cloves garlic, minced
1 yellow squash, cut into bite-size cubes
1 zucchini, cut into bite-size cubes
1 (12 oz.) package extra-firm tofu, cut into bite-size cubes
1/4 cup brown sugar
3 tbsps. soy sauce
1 tbsp. sriracha sauce
Salt and ground black pepper to taste

Directions:

1. Heat olive oil in a wok over medium-high heat.
2. Cook and stir garlic in hot oil until just fragrant, about 30 seconds.
3. Add squash and zucchini, cook and stir until vegetables soften, about 7 minutes. Transfer squash mixture to a bowl.
4. Place wok back over medium-high heat, place tofu pieces in the wok, and top with brown sugar and soy sauce.
5. Cook and stir until each side of tofu is golden brown, 3 to 5 minutes.
6. Return squash mixture to the wok; cook and stir until heated through, about 3 minutes.
7. Stir in Sriracha sauce and season with salt and black pepper.

Lime-Curry Tofu Stir-Fry

Ingredients:

2 tbsps. peanut oil
1 (16 oz.) package extra-firm tofu, cut into bite-sized cubes
1 tbsp. minced fresh ginger root
2 tbsps. red curry paste
1 lb. zucchini, diced
1 red bell pepper, diced
3 tbsps. lime juice
3 tbsps. soy sauce
2 tbsps. maple syrup
1 (14 oz.) can coconut milk
1/2 cup chopped fresh basil

Directions:

1. Heat the peanut oil in a wok over high heat.
2. Add the tofu and stir-fry until golden brown.
3. Remove the tofu and set aside, leaving the remaining oil in the wok.
4. Stir the ginger and curry paste into the hot oil for a few seconds until the curry paste is fragrant and the ginger begins to turn golden.
5. Add the zucchini and bell pepper; cook and stir for 1 minute.
6. Pour in the lime juice, soy sauce, maple syrup, coconut milk, and tofu.
7. Bring the coconut milk to a simmer, and cook a few minutes until the vegetables are tender and the tofu is hot.
8. Stir in the chopped basil just before serving.

Kung Pao Tofu Stir-Fry

Ingredients:

1 (16 oz.) package firm tofu, cut into 3 slices
1 cup low-sodium soy sauce, divided
1 (1 inch) piece ginger, finely grated
1 tbsp. canola oil
1 yellow onion, sliced
1 large green bell pepper, cut into chunks
2 small zucchini, chopped
6 small mushrooms, chopped
3 tbsps. rice wine vinegar
1 tbsp. Asian hot-chile sauce
2 tbsps. crushed roasted peanuts

Directions:

1. Lay tofu slices on a paper towel-lined plate and cover with more paper towels. Put a heavy object on top to press out excess water, about 15 minutes; drain and discard the accumulated liquid.
2. Mix 1/2 cup soy sauce and ginger in a large dish.
3. Add tofu slices and let marinate, about 15 minutes.
4. Preheat oven to 350 degrees F (175 degrees C). Line a baking sheet with parchment paper.
5. Flip tofu slices and let marinate on second side, about 15 minutes more.
6. Remove tofu from marinade and place on prepared baking sheet.
7. Bake in the preheated oven until dry, flipping once halfway through, about 40 minutes.
8. Cut into smaller pieces.
9. Heat oil in a wok over medium-high heat.
10. Add onion and green bell pepper; cook until onion is slightly translucent, 3 to 5 minutes.
11. Add zucchini and mushrooms; cook and stir until lightly browned, 2 to 3 minutes.
12. Stir in baked tofu.
13. Mix remaining 1/2 cup soy sauce, rice wine vinegar, and chile sauce in a small bowl.
14. Pour into the wok and stir until onion and tofu mixture is well-coated, about 1 minute. Garnish with roasted peanuts.

Spicy Tofu Stir Fry

Ingredients:

1/3 cup lite soy sauce
1 tbsp. Thai garlic chile paste
2 cloves garlic, diced
2 tsps. cayenne pepper
1 1/2 tsps. diced fresh ginger
1/2 (16 oz.) package linguine-style rice noodles
3 tbsps. olive oil
1 (12 oz.) package extra-firm tofu, cut into
1/2-inch cubes
3 green onions, minced
1 cup snow peas
1/2 green bell pepper, sliced
1/2 red bell pepper, sliced

Directions:

1. Whisk soy sauce, garlic chile paste, garlic, cayenne pepper, and ginger together in a small bowl until chile paste is completely dissolved.
2. Place noodles in a large bowl and cover with hot water. Set aside until noodles are softened, 8 to 10 minutes.
3. Drain and rinse.
4. Heat oil in a large wok over medium heat.
5. Cook and stir tofu cubes in hot oil until browned on all sides, 3 to 6 minutes.
6. Stir green onion into tofu; cook and stir until fragrant, about 2 minutes.
7. Pour 1/2 of the soy sauce mixture over tofu mixture; bring to a simmer and cook until sauce reduces, about 5 minutes.
8. Stir snow peas, green bell pepper, and red bell pepper into tofu mixture; cook and stir until vegetables are heated through, about 5 minutes.
9. Pour remaining soy sauce mixture over the top; cook and stir until liquid reduces and vegetables are tender yet still crisp to the bite, about 5 minutes.
10. Add rice noodles to tofu mixture and toss to coat; cook until noodles are heated through and flavors combine, 2 to 5 minutes.

Tofu Chanpuru

Ingredients:

1 (12 oz.) package extra-firm tofu, drained
1 (12 oz.) can fully cooked luncheon meat (such as SPAM), cubed
4 cloves garlic, chopped
1 tbsp. minced fresh ginger, or to taste
1/2 cup sake
1/2 cup miso paste
1/4 cup soy sauce
2 tbsps. white sugar
2 tsps. vegetable oil, or as needed
4 eggs, slightly beaten
2 tsps. vegetable oil, or as needed
1 large onion, chopped
1 head cabbage, cored and chopped
2 carrots, grated8 mushrooms, sliced
1 tbsp. chopped green onion, or more to taste

Directions:

1. Wrap tofu in a paper towel; cook in microwave for 1 minute. Squeeze extra water from tofu and wrap in a dry paper towel. Let sit to drain extra water, about 5 minutes.
2. Remove paper towel and cut tofu into cubes.
3. Combine luncheon meat, garlic, and ginger in a bowl. Whisk sake, miso paste, soy sauce, and sugar in a separate bowl.
4. Heat 2 tsps. vegetable oil in a wok over medium heat; cook and stir eggs until scrambled and cooked through, about 5 minutes. Transfer eggs to a plate.
5. Cook and stir tofu in the same wok until browned on all sides, 5 to 10 minutes. Transfer tofu to plate with eggs.
6. Cook and stir luncheon meat mixture in the same wok until cooked through and garlic is lightly browned, about 5 minutes.
7. Clean wok, then heat 2 tsps. vegetable oil over medium heat.
8. Cook and stir onion, cabbage, carrots, and mushrooms until onions are translucent and cabbage is softened, 10 to 12 minutes.
9. Add eggs, tofu, luncheon meat, and sake mixture to vegetable mixture; stir to coat.
10. Cook until heated through, about 1 minute.
11. Garnish with green onion.

Chinese Pepper Steak

Ingredients:

1 lb. beef top sirloin steak
1/4 cup soy sauce
2 tbsps. white sugar
2 tbsps. cornstarch
1/2 tsp. ground ginger
3 tbsps. vegetable oil, divided
1 red onion, cut into 1-inch squares
1 green bell pepper, cut into 1-inch squares
2 tomatoes, cut into wedges

Directions:

1. Slice the steak into 1/2-inch thick slices across the grain.
2. Whisk together soy sauce, sugar, cornstarch, and ginger in a bowl until the sugar has dissolved and the mixture is smooth.
3. Place the steak slices into the marinade, and stir until well-coated.
4. Heat 1 tbsp. of vegetable oil in a wok over medium-high heat, and place 1/3 of the steak strips into the hot oil.
5. Cook and stir until the beef is well-browned, about 3 minutes, and remove the beef from the wok to a bowl.
6. Repeat twice more, with the remaining beef, and set the cooked beef aside.
7. Return all the cooked beef to the hot wok, and stir in the onion.
8. Toss the beef and onion together until the onion begins to soften, about 2 minutes, then stir in the green pepper.
9. Cook and stir the mixture until the pepper has turned bright green and started to become tender, about 2 minutes, then add the tomatoes, stir everything together, and serve.

Pork and Shrimp Noodle Stir Fry

Ingredients:

1 (6.75 oz.) package rice noodles
5 tbsps. vegetable oil, divided
1 small onion, minced
2 cloves garlic, minced
1/2 tsp. ground ginger
1 1/2 cups cooked small shrimp, diced
1 1/2 cups chopped cooked pork
4 cups shredded bok choy
3 tbsps. oyster sauce
1/4 cup chicken broth
1/4 tsp. crushed red pepper flakes
1 green onion, minced

Directions:

1. Soak the rice noodles in warm water for 20 minutes; drain.
2. Heat 3 tbsps. oil in a wok over medium high heat. Saute noodles for 1 minute. Transfer to serving dish, and keep warm.
3. Add remaining 2 tbsps. oil to wok, and saute onion, garlic, ginger, shrimp and pork for 1 minute.
4. Stir in bok choy, oyster sauce and chicken broth.
5. Season with pepper flakes.
6. Cover, and cook for 1 minute, or until bok choy is wilted. Spoon over noodles, and garnish with minced green onion.

Szechuan Beef

Ingredients:

1 lb. sirloin steak, cut into bite size strips
1 tbsp. soy sauce
2 tsps. cornstarch
1/4 tsp. crushed red pepper
1 clove garlic, minced
2 tbsps. vegetable oil
3 cups fresh broccoli florets
2 small onions, cut into wedges
1 (8 oz.) can water chestnuts, drained
1/4 cup chicken broth
1/2 cup peanuts

Directions:

1. Toss beef with soy sauce, cornstarch, crushed red pepper and garlic in non-metal bowl.

2. Cover and refrigerate 20 minutes.
3. Heat oil in wok over high heat.
4. Stir fry beef until no longer pink, 5 minutes.
5. Stir in broccoli, onions and water chestnuts; cook 2 minutes.
6. Pour in broth, and bring to a boil.
7. Stir in peanuts, cook one minute more, and serve.

Moo Goo Gai Pan

Ingredients:

1 tbsp. vegetable oil
1/4 lb. sliced fresh mushrooms
1/4 lb. snow peas
1 (8 oz.) can sliced water chestnuts, drained
1/4 lb. sliced bok choy
Salt and black pepper to taste
1 tbsp. vegetable oil
1 tsp. minced garlic
1 tsp. minced fresh ginger root
3/4 cup chicken breast meat, thinly sliced
1 tsp. white wine
1/4 tsp. white sugar
1/4 cup chicken broth
1 tbsp. cornstarch
2 tbsps. water

Directions:

1. Heat 1 tbsp. of vegetable oil in a wok over high heat.
2. Stir in the mushrooms, snow peas, water chestnuts, and bok choy; season to taste with salt and pepper.
3. Cook and stir until the vegetables are just tender, about 5 minutes.
4. Remove the vegetables from the wok and wipe the wok clean.
5. Heat the remaining 1 tbsp. of vegetable oil in the wok.
6. Stir in the garlic and ginger; cook a few seconds until the garlic begins to turn golden brown.
7. Stir in the chicken and cook until the chicken is no longer pink, about 5 minutes.
8. Add the wine, sugar, and chicken broth; bring to a boil. Dissolve the cornstarch in the water and stir into the simmering sauce. Once the sauce returns to a simmer, stir until thick and clear, about 30 seconds. Return the vegetables to the wok and toss until hot and coated with the sauce.

Pork and Bamboo Shoots

Ingredients:

1 tbsp. peanut oil
1 (14 oz.) can thinly sliced bamboo shoots
2 tbsps. peanut oil
2 cloves garlic, minced
1 fresh red chile pepper, seeded and minced
1/2 tsp. crushed red pepper flakes
3 oz. ground pork
1 tsp. Shaoxing rice wine
Salt to taste
2 tsps. rice vinegar
2 tsps. soy sauce
3 tbsps. chicken broth
3 green onions, thinly sliced
1 tsp. sesame oil

Directions:

1. Heat one tbsp. peanut oil in a wok set over medium heat.
2. Add the bamboo shoots to the pan; stir-fry until dry and fragrant, about 3 minutes.
3. Remove from wok and reserve.
4. Increase temperature to high, and pour in the remaining peanut oil. Quickly fry the garlic, red chile, and red pepper flakes in the hot oil until fragrant.
5. Stir in the pork, and continue to stir-fry until it is cooked through.
6. Pour in the wine; season with salt to taste.
7. Return the bamboo shoots to the wok, and heat until sizzly.
8. Stir in the rice vinegar, soy sauce, chicken broth, and additional salt to taste.
9. Cook and stir for 1 to 2 minutes to allow the flavor to penetrate the bamboo shoots. At the end of cooking, stir in green onions.
10. Remove wok from heat; stir in sesame oil before serving.

Grapes and Rice Stir Fry

Ingredients:

1 tbsp. vegetable oil
1 cup sliced red grapes
1 cup cubed cooked chicken
2 cups cooked rice
1/4 cup chicken broth

Directions:

1. Heat the vegetable oil in a wok over medium high heat.
2. Stir in the grapes and chicken; cook and stir until the chicken is hot, and the grapes are tender, about 3 minutes.
3. Add the rice and chicken broth; continue cooking until the rice is hot, about 2 minutes more.

Vietnamese Stir-Fry

Ingredients:

1/4 cup olive oil
4 cloves garlic, minced
1 (1 inch) piece fresh ginger root, minced
1/4 cup fish sauce
1/4 cup soy sauce
1 dash sesame oil
2 lbs. sirloin tip, thinly sliced
1 tbsp. vegetable oil
2 cloves garlic, minced
3 green onions, cut into 2 inch pieces
1 large onion, thinly sliced
2 cups frozen whole green beans, partially thawed
1/2 cup beef broth
2 tbsps. lime juice
1 tbsp. chopped fresh Thai basil
1 tbsp. chopped fresh mint
1 pinch red pepper flakes, or to taste
1/2 tsp. ground black pepper
1/4 cup chopped fresh cilantro

Directions:

1. Whisk together the olive oil, 4 cloves of garlic, ginger, fish sauce, soy sauce, and sesame oil in a bowl, and pour into a resealable plastic bag.
2. Add the beef sirloin tip, coat with the marinade, squeeze out excess air, and seal the bag. Marinate in the refrigerator for 2 hours.
3. Remove the beef sirloin tip from the marinade, and shake off excess. Discard the remaining marinade.
4. Heat vegetable oil in a large wok over medium-high heat and stir in the beef.
5. Cook and stir until the beef is evenly browned, and no longer pink.
6. Place beef on a plate and set aside.
7. Reduce heat to medium, adding more vegetable oil to the wok if needed.
8. Stir in 2 cloves of garlic, green onion, and onion; cook and stir until the onion has softened and turned translucent, about 5 minutes.
9. Stir in green beans, beef broth, lime juice, basil, mint, red pepper flakes and pepper. Return beef sirloin to wok and toss to combine.
10. Remove from heat and toss in cilantro.

Spicy Crab Curry

Ingredients:

2 fresh Dungeness crabs, cleaned and shells cracked
2 tsps. ground turmeric
1/2 tsp. salt
1 tbsp. mustard seed
1 tbsp. hot water
1 tbsp. mustard oil
3 cups sliced red onion1
3/4 cups boiling potatoes, peeled, halved lengthwise, and sliced
2 whole cloves
1 (1 inch) piece cinnamon stick
2 pods green cardamom pods
5 whole black peppercorns
2 large tomatoes, coarsely chopped
4 Thai green chiles
1 1/2 tsps. garlic paste
1 1/2 tsps. ginger paste
1 tsp. cayenne pepper
Salt to taste
1 tsp. white sugar

Garnish Ingredients:

1 wedge fresh lemon
1/2 cup chopped fresh cilantro

Directions:

1. Rub the crabs with 1 tsp. of the turmeric and 1/2 tsp. salt; let them marinate for 1 hour.
2. Combine the mustard seed and hot water in a small bowl and let stand for 10 minutes. Use a mortar and pestle to grind the seeds into a coarse paste.
3. Heat the oil in a wok over medium heat.
4. Add the crabs and stir fry until they change color, about 4 minutes.
5. Remove the crabs from the oil and set aside.
6. Add the sliced onions to the wok and cook and stir over medium heat until the onions are translucent, about 5 minutes. Raise the heat to high, add the potatoes, and cook, stirring constantly, for about 2 minutes.
7. Add the cloves, cinnamon stick, cardamom pods, and peppercorns, and stir for thirty seconds.
8. Stir in the tomatoes, ginger paste, and garlic paste. Halve three of the chiles and add them to the wok.
9. Cook and stir for an additional minute or two over high heat.
10. Reduce the heat to medium; add the remaining 1 tsp. turmeric, the cayenne pepper, and the mustard paste and stir to combine.
11. Add the crabs to the wok and pour in just enough water to cover the vegetables.
12. Bring the water to a boil and stir in the sugar and salt to taste.
13. Cover the wok, reduce the heat, and simmer until the potatoes are tender and the water is reduced by half, about 10 minutes.
14. Remove the lid, stir, and simmer until the gravy is thickened, about 5 minutes more.
15. Squeeze the lemon wedge over the finished dish. Garnish with chopped cilantro and sliced green chile and serve hot, with rice.

Curry Tofu Stir-Fry

Ingredients:

Cooking spray
1 lb. extra-firm tofu, cut into 1-inch cubes
1 tbsp. vegetable oil
1 cup sliced fresh mushrooms
1 tbsp. chopped garlic
3 cups fresh spinach
2 tbsps. soy sauce
1 1/2 tbsps. curry powder
1 tsp. red pepper flakes

Directions:

1. Preheat oven to 400 degrees F (200 degrees C). Spray a baking sheet with baking spray; arrange tofu in a single layer.
2. Bake tofu in preheated oven until evenly browned, flipping after 10 minutes, about 20 minutes total.
3. Heat vegetable oil in a wok over medium-high heat.
4. Add mushrooms and garlic; cook and stir until mushrooms are tender; 2 to 3 minutes.
5. Add tofu, spinach, soy sauce, and curry powder; cook and stir until spinach is wilted; 3 to 5 minutes.
6. Sprinkle red pepper flakes over mixture.

Pad Thai with Spaghetti Squash

Ingredients:

1 (12 oz.) package extra-firm tofu
1 spaghetti squash, halved lengthwise
6 tbsps. sesame oil, divided
2 eggs
1/4 cup cornstarch
2 cups bean sprouts
6 tbsps. pad Thai sauce
1 tbsp. Thai garlic chile paste
4 green onions, thinly sliced
1 cup cashew pieces

Directions:

1. Drain tofu and slice horizontally into 1/4-inch slices. Lay paper towels on a cutting board, place tofu slices on top, and cover with another layer of paper towels.
2. Place something heavy, such as a cast iron skillet, on top. Allow to drain for 1 to 2 hours.
3. Preheat oven to 450 degrees F (230 degrees C).
4. Place spaghetti squash, cut-side up, on a baking sheet.
5. Bake spaghetti squash in preheated oven until tender, 45 to 50 minutes.
6. Remove squash from oven; remove and separate strands from peel using a fork.
7. Heat 2 tbsps. sesame oil in wok over medium-high heat.
8. Add eggs, cook and stir until eggs are cooked through and scrambles, about 5 minutes. Transfer eggs to a plate.
9. Cut each slice of tofu into 9 triangles and place in a bowl; add cornstarch and toss to coat. Shake tofu to remove excess cornstarch.

10. Heat remaining 4 tbsps. sesame oil in wok over medium-high heat; add tofu and saute until crispy, about 5 minutes.
11. Remove from wok.
12. Place squash, bean sprouts, Pad Thai sauce, garlic chile paste, and onions into wok and saute until heated through, about 10 minutes.
13. Mix tofu and scrambled eggs into squash mixture.
14. Remove wok from heat, add cashews, and toss to combine.

Honey and Ginger Chicken

Ingredients:

2 tbsps. olive oil
2 large boneless, skinless chicken breasts, cubed
1/4 cup honey
2 tbsps. finely chopped ginger
2 red bell peppers, chopped
1 large onion, cut into 8 wedges
1 large head broccoli, cut into florets
1 cup peeled and cubed fresh pineapple
1/2 cup honey

Directions:

1. Heat olive oil in a wok over medium heat.
2. Add chicken cubes, 1/4 cup honey, and ginger.
3. Cook and stir until chicken is golden brown, about 10 minutes.
4. Add bell peppers, onion, broccoli, pineapple, and remaining 1/2 cup honey.
5. Cover and cook over medium-high heat until vegetables are tender, 5 to 10 minutes, stirring occasionally.

Thai Ginger Chicken (Gai Pad King)

Ingredients:

1 1/2 cups uncooked jasmine rice
3 1/2 cups water
2 tbsps. vegetable oil
3 cloves garlic, minced
1 lb. chicken breast halves, cut into thin strips
1 tbsp. Asian fish sauce
1 tbsp. oyster sauce
1 tbsp. white sugar
1/2 cup fresh ginger, cut into matchsticks
1 large red bell pepper, cut into strips
3/4 cup sliced fresh mushrooms
4 green onions cut into 2-inch pieces
1/2 tsp. Thai red chile paste, or to taste
2 tbsps. chicken broth
Salt and ground black pepper to taste
2 tbsps. fresh cilantro leaves

Directions:

1. Bring the rice and water to a boil in a saucepan.
2. Reduce heat to medium-low; cover and simmer until the rice is tender and the liquid has been absorbed, 20 to 25 minutes.
3. Meanwhile, heat a wok over medium-high heat.
4. Stir in the garlic and chicken; cook for 2 minutes.
5. Add the fish sauce, oyster sauce, sugar, ginger, red pepper, mushrooms, and onions.
6. Cook and stir until the chicken is no longer pink and the vegetables are nearly tender, about 3 minutes. Dissolve the chile paste in the chicken broth, then add to the chicken mixture.
7. Season to taste with salt and pepper; sprinkle with cilantro leaves to garnish. Serve with the hot rice.

Singapore Noodles

Ingredients:

6 dry Chinese egg noodle nests
1/4 cup peanut oil
6 cloves garlic, minced
2 tbsps. slivered fresh ginger
2 tsps. crushed red pepper flakes
1 lb. skinless, boneless chicken breast halves
1/3 cup green onions, chopped
2/3 cup julienned carrot
1 (8 oz.) can sliced water chestnuts, drained
2 (15 oz.) cans whole straw mushrooms, drained
1/4 cup peanut butter
1/4 cup oyster sauce
3 tbsps. curry powder
2 tsps. soy sauce

Directions:

1. Bring a large pot of lightly-salted water to a rolling boil; add the egg noodle nests and return to a boil. Turn off the heat and let stand for 5 minutes; drain and set aside.
2. Heat the peanut oil in a wok over high heat.
3. Stir in the garlic, ginger, and red pepper flakes; cook a few seconds until the garlic begins to turn golden.
4. Add the chicken, green onions, and carrots.
5. Cook and stir until the chicken is no longer pink, about 5 minutes.
6. Stir in the water chestnuts, mushrooms, peanut butter, oyster sauce, curry powder, and soy sauce until the peanut butter has dissolved into the sauce.
7. Stir the noodles into the chicken mixture; cover and reduce heat to warm or very low. Let stand 10 to 15 minutes for the noodles to absorb some of the sauce.

Okinawan-Style Pad Thai

Ingredients:

1/2 cup rice wine vinegar
1/2 cup white sugar
1/4 cup oyster sauce
2 tbsps. tamarind pulp
1 (12 oz.) package dried rice noodles
Cold water, as needed
1/2 cup peanut oil
4 eggs
1 1/2 tsps. minced garlic
12 oz. chicken breast, cut into 1/2-inch strips
1 1/2 tbsps. white sugar, or more to taste
1 1/2 tsps. salt
1 1/2 cups dry-roasted, unsalted peanuts
1 1/2 tsps. dried ground Asian radish
1 tsp. chili powder
1/2 cup chopped fresh chives
2 cups fresh bean sprouts
1 lime, cut into wedges

Directions:

1. Whisk together rice wine vinegar, 1/2 cup sugar, oyster sauce, and tamarind pulp in a saucepan over medium heat until sugar dissolves, about 5 minutes; remove from heat and set aside.
2. Place rice noodles in a large bowl and pour enough cold water to cover noodles. Allow to soften, about 10 minutes.
3. Drain.
4. Heat peanut oil in a wok over medium heat.
5. Cook and stir eggs and garlic in hot oil until eggs are softly cooked, 2 to 3 minutes.
6. Stir chicken and noodles into eggs and cook until chicken is no longer pink in the center and juices run clear, about 5 minutes.
7. Pour rice wine vinegar sauce, 1 1/2 tbsps. sugar, and 1 1/2 tsps. salt into the noodle mixture.
8. Stir peanuts, ground radish, and chili powder into noodle mixture.
9. Cook until peanuts soften slightly, about 5 minutes.
10. Add more sugar or chili powder if desired.
11. Remove from heat and toss chives with noodle mixture.
12. Top with bean sprouts and garnish with lime wedges.

Thai Beef with a Tangerine Sauce

Ingredients:

1 (8 oz.) package dry Chinese noodles
1/4 cup hoisin sauce
1/4 cup dry sherry
1 tsp. tangerine zest
1/4 tsp. ground ginger
4 tsp. vegetable oil
1 pound flank beef steak, cut diagonally into 2 inch strips
2 tsp. vegetable oil
1/2 small butternut squash, peeled, seeded, and thinly sliced
1 cup sliced fresh mushrooms
1 large red onion, cut into 2 inch strips
3 cup cabbage, thinly sliced
1 tangerine, sectioned and seeded

Directions:

1. Fill a large pot with lightly salted water and bring to a rolling boil over high
2. heat. Once the water is boiling, stir in the noodles, and return to a boil.
3. Cook the pasta uncovered, stirring occasionally, until the pasta has cooked
4. through, but is still firm to the bite, about 5 minutes.
5. Drain, rinse, and set aside.
6. Whisk together the hoisin sauce, sherry, tangerine zest, and ground ginger in a small bowl.
7. Heat 2 tsps. vegetable oil in a large wok over high heat.
8. Add one half of the beef slices to the pan; cook, stirring constantly, until the
9. meat is nicely browned, 2 to 3 minutes.
10. Remove meat to a platter with a slotted spoon.
11. Repeat with the remaining beef.
12. Heat the remaining 2 tsps. of oil in the pan.
13. Stir in the butternut squash, mushrooms, and onion.
14. Cook, stirring constantly, until vegetables
15. are crisp-tender and slightly brown on the edges, 5 to 7 minutes.
16. Add the cabbage, and cook and stir until slightly wilted, about 2 additional minutes.
17. Reduce the heat to medium.
18. Stir the cooked beef, tangerine sections, and hoisin mixture into the vegetables.
19. Cook until heated through, 2 to 3 minutes.
20. Serve over Chinese noodles.

Pork, Apple, and Ginger Stir-Fry

Ingredients:

2 tbsps. hoisin sauce
2 tbsps. brown sugar
6 tbsps. soy sauce
1/2 cup applesauce
1 lb. pork loin, sliced and cut into thin strips
1 1/2 tbsps. cornstarch
2 tbsps. peanut oil
1/2 tsp. sesame oil
1 tbsp. chopped fresh ginger root
3 cups broccoli florets

Directions:

1. Whisk together the hoisin sauce, brown sugar, soy sauce, and applesauce in a small bowl; set aside.
2. Combine the pork and cornstarch in a bowl.
3. Mix until the cornstarch evenly coats the pork; set aside.
4. Heat the peanut oil and sesame oil in a wok over medium-high heat.
5. Cook the pork in three separate batches in the hot oil until no longer pink in the middle, 2 to 3 minutes per batch.
6. Remove pork to a plate lined with paper towels to drain, reserving the oil.
7. Add the ginger to the wok; cook and stir for 30 seconds.
8. Stir in the broccoli and cook until tender. Return the pork to the wok and pour in the sauce; toss to coat.
9. Cook until all ingredients are hot.

Crab Rangoon

Ingredients:

1 quart oil for frying
1 tbsp. vegetable oil
1 clove garlic, minced
2 tbsps. minced onion
1 medium head bok choy, chopped
2 tbsps. chopped snow peas
1 (6 oz.) can crab meat, drained
1 (8 oz.) package cream cheese, softened
1 tbsp. soy sauce
1 (14 oz.) package small won ton wrappers

Directions:

1. Heat oil for frying in deep-fryer or large, heavy saucepan to 375 degrees F (190 degrees C).
2. Heat 1 tbsp. vegetable oil in a large wok.
3. Add garlic and onion, and saute for 2 minutes.
4. Add bok choy and pea pods, and stir fry until the bok choy and pea pods are crisp-tender.
5. In a large mixing bowl, combine crab, cream cheese, soy sauce and sauteed vegetable mixture. Drop mixture by 3/4 tsp. into the center of a won ton wrapper. Fold the wrapper in half to make a triangle. Seal the wrapper around the mixture by wetting your finger with cold water and pressing the ends together.
6. In batches, fry the dumplings in the prepared oil until golden brown.
7. Drain on paper towels.

Chinese Dong'an Chicken

Ingredients:

1 (2 lb.) whole chicken
1 tbsp. cornstarch
1 tbsp. cold water
6 tbsps. peanut oil
1 1/2 tbsps. grated fresh ginger
2 tsps. finely chopped dried chile peppers
3 tbsps. vinegar
1 1/2 tbsps. rice wine
20 Szechuan peppercorns, crushed
Salt to taste
2 spring onions, chopped, or more to taste
1/8 tsp. monosodium glutamate (MSG)
2 tsps. sesame oil

Directions:

1. Place chicken in a stockpot with water to cover.
2. Bring to a boil and cook until juices run clear, at least 20 minutes. An instant-read thermometer inserted into the thickest part of the thigh near the bone should read 165 degrees F (74 degrees C).
3. Remove chicken.
4. Set aside to cool. Reserve 1/2 cup of the cooking liquid.
5. Remove chicken meat from bone.
6. Cut meat into 1/2-inch by 2-inch strips.
7. Mix cornstarch and cold water together in a small bowl.
8. Toss meat in 1/2 of the cornstarch mixture.
9. Heat peanut oil in a wok over high heat.
10. Add chicken mixture, ginger, and chiles; cook and stir until fragrant, 2 to 3 minutes.
11. Add reserved cooking liquid, vinegar, rice wine, peppercorns, and salt. Return to boil; cook and stir until mixture is almost dry, about 3 minutes.
12. Stir in spring onions, monosodium glutamate, and remaining cornstarch mixture; cook until sauce is thickened, 2 to 3 minutes more. Drizzle with sesame oil.

Pad Thai Quinoa

Ingredients:

4 cups chicken broth
2 cups quinoa, rinsed and drained
1 tbsp. coconut oil, divided
1 large chicken breast, cut into thin strips
3/4 cup shredded cabbage
1/2 cup edamame
1/4 cup diced broccoli stems
2 carrots, cut into matchsticks
2 green onions, chopped
3 eggs
1 tsp. sesame oil

Thai Peanut Sauce Ingredients:

1/4 cup natural peanut butter
1/4 cup soy sauce
3 tbsps. rice vinegar
2 tbsps. chili garlic sauce
2 tbsps. chopped fresh ginger
3 cloves garlic, minced
1 tsp. sesame oil
1/2 cup salted peanuts, chopped
3 tbsps. chopped fresh cilantro

Directions:

1. Bring chicken broth and quinoa to a boil in a saucepan.
2. Reduce heat to medium-low, cover, and simmer until quinoa is tender, 15 to 20 minutes. Set aside.
3. Heat 1 1/2 tsps. coconut oil in a wok over medium-high heat.
4. Add chicken; stir until cooked through; about 5 minutes.
5. Remove chicken from wok. Heat remaining 1 1/2 tsps. coconut oil.
6. Add cabbage, edamame, broccoli, carrot, and green onions and saute until vegetables soften slightly, 2 to 3 minutes.
7. Whisk eggs with sesame oil in a small bowl. Push vegetables to the sides of the wok to make a well in the center; pour eggs in and stir to scramble, about 3 minutes.
8. Combine peanut butter, soy sauce, rice vinegar, chili garlic sauce, ginger, garlic, and sesame oil together in a small bowl.
9. Pour Thai peanut sauce over vegetable and egg mixture in the wok.
10. Return chicken to the wok and add quinoa; mix well to combine.
11. Stir in chopped peanuts and cilantro and serve.

Zucchini Noodles Pad Thai

Ingredients:

3 large zucchini
1/4 cup chicken stock
2 1/2 tbsps. tamarind paste
2 tbsps. soy sauce
2 tbsps. oyster sauce
1 1/2 tbsps. Asian chile pepper sauce
1 tbsp. Worcestershire sauce
1 tbsp. fresh lime juice
1 tbsp. white sugar
2 tbsps. sesame oil
1 tbsp. chopped garlic
12 oz. chicken breasts, cut into 1-inch cubes
8 oz. peeled and deveined shrimp
2 eggs, beaten
2 tbsps. water, or as needed
3 cups bean sprouts, divided
6 green onions, chopped into 1-inch pieces
2 tbsps. chopped unsalted dry-roasted peanuts
1/4 cup chopped fresh basil

Directions:

1. Make zucchini noodles using a spiralizer.
2. Whisk chicken stock, tamarind paste, soy sauce, oyster sauce, chile pepper sauce, Worcestershire sauce, lime juice, and sugar together in a small bowl to make a smooth sauce.
3. Heat sesame oil in a wok over high heat.
4. Add garlic and stir until fragrant, about 10 seconds.
5. Add chicken and shrimp; cook and stir until chicken is no longer pink in the center and the juices run clear, 5 to 7 minutes.
6. Push chicken and shrimp to the sides of the wok to make a space in the center.
7. Pour eggs and scramble until firm, 2 to 3 minutes.
8. Add zucchini noodles and sauce; cook and stir, adding water if needed, about 3 minutes.
9. Add 2 cups bean sprouts and green onions; cook and stir until combined, 1 to 2 minutes.
10. Remove wok from heat and sprinkle peanuts over noodles. Serve garnished with remaining 1 cup bean sprouts and fresh basil.

Goong Tod Kratiem Prik Thai

Ingredients:

8 cloves garlic, chopped, or more to taste
2 tbsps. tapioca flour
2 tbsps. fish sauce
2 tbsps. light soy sauce
1 tbsp. white sugar
1/2 tsp. ground white pepper
1/4 cup vegetable oil, divided, or as needed
1 lb. whole unpeeled prawns, divided

Directions:

1. Combine garlic, tapioca flour, fish sauce, soy sauce, sugar, and white pepper in a bowl.
2. Add prawns and toss to coat.
3. Heat 2 tbsps. oil in a wok over high heat.
4. Add 1/2 of the prawns in single layer.
5. Fry until golden brown and crispy, 1 to 2 minutes per side.
6. Repeat with remaining oil and remaining prawns.

Spicy Shrimp Stir-Fry

Ingredients:

1/2 cup lemon juice
1 small onion, finely chopped
1/2 cup olive oil
3 cloves garlic, minced
1 tbsp. lemon zest
1 tbsp. grated ginger
1 tsp. ground turmeric
24 large shrimp, peeled and deveined
1 tbsp. coconut oil, or as needed

Directions:

1. Mix together lemon juice, onion, olive oil, garlic, lemon zest, ginger, and turmeric in a bowl.
2. Place shrimp into marinade, cover, and refrigerate shrimp and marinade mixture overnight.
3. Remove shrimp, saving the marinade. Heat a wok over medium-high heat; melt coconut oil in hot wok.
4. Stir-fry shrimp in coconut oil until shrimp are opaque and pink, 5 to 10 minutes.
5. Add reserved marinade and bring to a boil, stirring constantly.

Paella

Ingredients:

5 (4 oz.) links hot Italian sausage, cut into 1 inch pieces
5 (4 oz.) links mild Italian sausage, cut into 1 inch pieces
15 raw chicken tenders or strips
2 lbs. large shrimp - peeled and deveined
1 onion, chopped
1 green bell pepper, seeded and cut into strips
1 large stalk celery, with leaves, finely chopped
2 cloves garlic, minced (optional)
2 cups uncooked long grain rice
2 (14.5 oz.) cans peeled and diced tomatoes, juice reserved
2 bay leaves
2 tsps. salt
1 tsp. dried oregano
3/4 tsp. ground turmeric
3 1/2 cups chicken broth

Directions:

1. Heat a wok over medium-high heat. Fry hot and mild Italian sausage pieces in the wok until brown on all sides.
2. Remove sausage, and fry the chicken strips in the sausage drippings until browned.
3. Remove chicken and saute onions, green pepper, celery, and garlic for 5 minutes, or until tender.
4. Stir in the uncooked rice, tomatoes, bay leaves, salt, oregano and turmericup
5. Cook and stir for 1 minute, then mix in the reserved tomato juice and chicken broth.
6. Add chicken pieces, cover and simmer for about 20 minutes.
7. Add sausage to the mixture, and continue to simmer for 15 minutes, then stir in the shrimp; cover and cook for 5 to 10 more minutes, or until shrimp is cooked through.

Green Curry Sweet Potato and Aubergine (Eggplant)

Ingredients:

1 tbsp. vegetable oil
1 onion, chopped
1 tbsp. green curry paste, or more to taste
1 eggplant, quartered and sliced
1 (14 oz.) can coconut milk
1 cup vegetable stock
1 sweet potato, peeled and sliced
6 kaffir lime leaves
2 tbsps. lime juice
2 tsps. lime zest
2 tsps. soft brown sugarsalt
1 shredded kaffir lime leaf for garnish
1 sprig chopped fresh cilantro for garnish

Directions:

1. Heat oil in a large wok over medium heat.
2. Add onion and curry paste; cook and stir until fragrant, about 3 minutes.
3. Stir in eggplant; cook until softened, 4 to 5 minutes.
4. Pour coconut milk and vegetable stock onto the eggplant mixture.
5. Bring to a boil; reduce heat and simmer until heated through, about 5 minutes.
6. Stir in sweet potato and lime leaves; cook and stir until vegetables are tender, about 10 minutes.
7. Mix in lime juice, lime zest, and brown sugar; stir until combined.
8. Season with salt; garnish with shredded lime leaf and cilantro.

Sweet Potato, Spinach, and Halloumi Curry

Ingredients:

2 large sweet potatoes, peeled and chopped
1 (14.5 oz.) can diced tomatoes
3 tsps. curry powder
2 tsps. chili powder
1 tsp. ground cumin
1 (14 oz.) can coconut milk
1 (8 oz.) package fresh spinach
1/2 diced green chile pepper, or to taste
1 cube vegetable bouillon
2 tsps. chili jam
1 (8.8 oz.) package halloumi cheese, sliced
1 (7 oz.) can chickpeas, drained

Directions:

1. Place sweet potatoes into a large pot and cover with water; bring to a boil.
2. Cook until tender, about 6 minutes.
3. Drain.
4. Combine sweet potatoes, tomatoes, curry powder, chili powder, and cumin in a saucepan over medium heat and bring to a simmer.
5. Add coconut milk, spinach, chile pepper, bouillon cube, and chili jam. Simmer until curry starts to thicken and has cooked down a little, 15 to 20 minutes.
6. Meanwhile, fry halloumi in a wok over medium heat until browned, 4 to 6 minutes.
7. Add cooked halloumi and chickpeas to curry and heat through, about 5 minutes.

Tangy Pepperoni and Cashew Pork

Ingredients:

1 tbsp. vegetable oil
2 boneless pork chops
2 cloves garlic, minced
1/2 onion, cut into chunks
1/2 green bell pepper, chopped
1 sprig fresh basil for garnish
1/3 cup chicken broth
1/2 cup white wine
1 tbsp. tomato paste
1 dash Worcestershire sauce
1 pinch dried thyme
1 pinch dried parsley
Salt and pepper to taste
1/2 cup chopped pepperoni
1 tomato, chopped
1/3 cup cashews

Directions:

1. Heat the oil in a wok over medium-high heat, and evenly brown the pork chops. Set aside.
2. Mix the garlic, onion, and green pepper into the wok, and cook until tender.
3. Stir in the chicken broth, wine, and tomato paste.
4. Mix in Worcestershire sauce, thyme, parsley, salt, and pepper.
5. Cook until heated through, then stir in pepperoni.
6. Return chops to wok.
7. Cover wok, and continue cooking 15 minutes over medium heat, until sauce has thickened and pork chops are cooked to desired doneness.
8. Mix in the tomato and cashews, and cook until heated through. Scoop sauce over chops and garnish with basil sprigs to serve.

Caribbean Jerk Stir Fry

Ingredients:

1 tbsp. vegetable oil
1 green bell pepper, seeded and cubed
1 red bell pepper, seeded and cubed
1/4 cup sliced sweet onions
3/4 lb. chicken breast, cut into strips
2 1/2 tsps. Caribbean jerk seasoning
1/2 cup plum sauce
1 tbsp. soy sauce
1/4 cup chopped roasted peanuts

Directions:

1. Heat the oil in a large wok over medium-high heat.
2. Cook and stir the bell pepper and onion in the oil until slightly tender, 5 to 7 minutes.
3. Remove pepper and onion from the wok and set aside.
4. Add the chicken to the wok; season with jerk seasoning; cook and stir chicken until no longer pink inside.
5. Pour the plum sauce in with the chicken; add the bell peppers and onions; toss to combine.
6. Cook until the peppers and onions are heated completely, 3 to 5 minutes.
7. Sprinkle with soy sauce and chopped peanuts to serve.

Rice Dumplings

Ingredients:

2 cups of cooked rice
7 tbsps. soy sauce
Sesame seed oil (for frying the rice)
water (for boiling dumplings)
1 tbsp. sesame seeds
1 cup wheat starch
1/4 tsp. salt
1 cup boiling water
1 tbsp. lard

Directions:

1. Place wheat starch into a medium bowl. Sift in salt. Slowly pour in the boiling water.
2. Pour in only as much as you need.
3. Stir until you have a sticky dough. Let the dough rest and cool for 30 minutes.
4. Add the tbsp. of lard to the dough, a portion at a time, gradually working it in. Knead the dough until it is smooth and satiny.
5. Make sure the lard is fully mixed in, then place it off to the side.
6. Pour the sesame seed oil into a wok and turn the heat on high. When the oil is bubbling, pour in the rice.
7. Fry the rice, gradually adding soy sauce until it is a yellow color.
8. Pour in the sesame seeds for flavor. Let the rice cool.
9. While the rice is cooling, place squares of dumpling dough on a cooking sheet, leaving a little more than half off the side.
10. Once the rice is cool, ball it and place a reasonably sized ball onto each of the squares of dough.
11. Form slightly bigger squares with the remaining dough and lay them on top of the rice. Use a fork to press the edges of the top and bottom dough together.
12. Boil until all dumplings have risen to the top of the water.

Charleston Chicken And Rice

Ingredients:

1 tbsp. oil
1/4 cup minced green onions
1 cup long grain rice
1 cup chicken broth
1 cup water
1 1/2 tsp. paprika
1/4 tsp. pepper
1/2 tsp. salt
2 cup diced cooked chicken or turkey
1 tbsp. sauce diable or 1 tsp. Worcestershire sauce and 1 tsp. prepared mustard
2 tbsp. chunky peanut butter

Directions:

1. Heat oil in Wok.
2. Add onions and stir fry until soft.
3. Stir in rice until grains are coated with oil.
4. Pour in broth and water, add paprika, pepper and salt.
5. Stir only until blended.
6. Bring to boil, add peanut butter, cover and reduce heat. Simmer until rice is tender and almost all liquid has been absorbed.
7. Add chicken, stir gently to blend.
8. Remove Wok from heat and let stand covered for about 10 minutes.
9. Stir in sauce diable or Worcestershire sauce with mustard. If necessary return Wok to low heat, toss and stir gently with a fork until reheated.
10. Makes 6 servings.

Creamed Cabbage

Ingredients:

2 tbsp. butter
1/8 tsp. ground ginger
6 cup sliced cabbage
1 tbsp. flour
1/3 cup milk
2 tbsp. pimiento, chopped
1 tsp. instant chicken bouillon granules

Directions:

1. Melt butter in Wok.
2. Stir fry cabbage and ginger about 3 minutes.
3. Stir in flour.
4. Add milk, pimiento, and bouillon.
5. Cook and stir until thick and bubbly. Then cook and stir 1 minute longer. Serve at once.

Clam And Cheese Spaghetti

Ingredients:

2 (6 oz.) cans minced clams
1 tbsp. oil
3 green onions, thinly sliced
1 clove garlic, minced
1 tbsp. flour
1/2 tsp. basil
1 cup milk
2 tsp. parsley
1/4 cup Parmesan cheese
1/2 tsp. salt
8 oz. spaghetti, cooked and drained

Directions:

1. Drain clams, save 1/2 cup liquid. Heat wok on high.
2. Add oil, stir fry onions and garlic 2 minutes.
3. Stir in flour.
4. Add milk and clam juice.
5. Cook until slightly thick and bubbly.
6. Cook 1 minute longer.
7. Add clams, parsley, salt and basil and pepper.
8. Cook 2 minutes.
9. Add cooked spaghetti and cheese.
10. Toss - heat through. Serve. 4 to 5 servings.

Spicy Poached Pears

Ingredients:

3/4 cup dry white wine
1/3 cup orange juice
1/4 cup packed brown sugar
1 tsp. ground cinnamon
6 lg. pears, peeled, halved and cored or canned pears
Ice cream

Directions:

1. In Wok cook and stir over medium heat wine, juice, sugar and cinnamon until sugar dissolves.
2. Add pear halves; cover and cook 8 to 10 minutes or until almost tender. Uncover and cook about 20 minutes longer, stirring often. Cool. If using canned pears, heat through.
3. Serve warm with ice cream.

Stir Fried Liver

Ingredients:

1/2 lb. partially frozen liver, cut in strips
2 slices ginger root, minced
2 tsp. cornstarch
2 tbsp. cooking sherry
1 tbsp. soy sauce
1/2 tsp. sugar
2 tbsp. oil
2 scallions or onions, chopped
1 clove garlic, minced
1/2 tbsp. salt

Vegetable Ingredients:

2 cups combination peas, green beans, celery, carrots, green peppers, mushrooms, bok choy

Directions:

1. Combine ginger root, cornstarch, sherry, soy sauce and sugar.
2. Add to liver. Let stand 20 minutes. Heat oil in wok.
3. Add scallions, garlic, salt and vegetables.
4. Stir fry just until vegetables are crisp tender.
5. Remove.
6. Add liver and stir fry 2 to 3 minutes. Return cooked vegetables to liver and stir to reheat. Serve over rice.

Seafood With Rice

Ingredients:

1 oz. snow peas
1/2 oz. Chinese potato
1 oz. fresh carrots
1 oz. sliced bamboo
1 oz. celery
3 scallops
2 shrimp (21/25 size)
3 oz. fresh fish, cut in 1/3
8 oz. stock
2 tbsp. peanut oil
Pinch garlic
Pinch ginger
1 tsp. shoyu
1/4 tsp. sesame oil
1 tsp. oyster sauce

1/2 tsp. salt
Dash ajinomoto
1/2 tsp. sugar
2 each crab claws
3 oz. saimin noodles
5 oz. rice pilaf
Fresh parsley

Directions:

1. Deep fry raw noodles in round basket shape and set aside on platter. Heat wok and add ginger, garlic, scallops, shrimp, and fresh fish. Fry until the fish is almost cooked.
2. Add all the vegetables and stir-fry for 3 minutes.
3. Add shoyu, sesame oil, oyster sauce, salt, ajinomoto, and sugar.
4. Put mixture on fried noodles, add crab claws on each side of mixture. Rice for starch and garnish with fresh parsley.

Party Peach Sauce

Ingredients:

2 lbs. fresh peaches, remove pits, peel, slice
1/3 cup sugar
1/4 cup water
1/4 cup lemon juice
1/4 tsp. ground nutmeg
1/4 cup sliced almonds
1/4 cup peach brandy or plain brandy
Vanilla ice cream

Directions:

1. In a large wok mix sugar, water, juice and nutmeg.
2. Bring to boiling.
3. Add peaches.
4. Stir and reduce heat.
5. Cover and simmer about 10 minutes or until peaches are tender.
6. Stir every so often. Then stir in almonds and brandy. Serve warm over ice cream.

Pork Fajitas

Ingredients:

1 lb. lean boneless pork
2 cloves garlic, minced
1 tsp. oregano, crumbled
1/2 tsp. cumin
1 tsp. seasoned salt
2 tbsp. orange juice
2 tbsp. vinegar
Dash of hot pepper sauce
1 tbsp. cooking oil
Flour tortillas
Optional Toppings:
1 green pepper, peeled & sliced
1 med. onion, peeled & sliced
Shredded lettuce
Shredded cheese
Diced tomatoes
Bottled salsa

Directions:

1. Slice pork across grain into 1/8 inch strips (much easier if partially frozen). Marinate pork strips in garlic, oregano, cumin, salt, orange juice, vinegar and hot pepper sauce for 15 minutes to 2 hours.
2. Heat wok (400 degrees F).
3. Add tbsp. of oil and pork strips; stir fry until pork is no longer pink about 5-8 minutes. Serve in heated flour tortillas, with options.

Chicken And Peaches

Ingredients:

2 (8 oz.) boneless chicken breast, skinned
1 green pepper
1 yellow pepper
1 carrot
3 tbsp. teriyaki sauce
2 tbsp. oil
1 cup brown rice
1 red pepper
2 celery stalks
1 (16 oz.) canned sliced peaches
1 tsp. apple pie spice or cinnamon

Directions:

1. Slice chicken breast in 1/2 inch strips, marinate with 1/2 of juice from peaches and 1/2 peaches, 1 tbsp. teriyaki sauce, 1/2 tsp. apple pie spice. Marinate for at least 1 hour or up to 24 hours.
2. Slice peppers, celery and carrot in long strips. Marinate vegetables with other 1/2 of peaches and juice, 1 tbsp. teriyaki and 1/2 tsp. apple pie spice for at least 1 hour.
3. Cook rice according to directions on box. Heat Wok.
4. Add 1 tbsp. oil, cook chicken with marinate on high stirring constantly for 2-3 minutes.
5. Remove chicken, set aside.
6. Cook vegetables and peaches with marinate in Wok 2-3 minutes until celery is translucent.
7. Add chicken to vegetables, cook together covered on low 5 minutes, stirring occasionally.
8. Remove from Wok.
9. Place in covered casserole to keep warm.
10. Turn Wok on high, add 1 tbsp. oil.
11. Stir rice into Wok and 1 tbsp. teriyaki and 1/4 cup juice from chicken.
12. Cook, stirring constantly for 3 minutes.
13. Remove from wok.
14. Place in covered casserole. Serve chicken and vegetables over bed of rice.

Vegetable Chili

Ingredients:

2 tbsp. cooking oil
1 med. onion, chopped
1 stalk celery, sliced
1 med. zucchini or yellow summer squash, sliced
1 1/2 tsp. chili powder
1 tsp. worcestershire sauce
1/4 tsp. ground red pepper
1 (15 oz.) can red kidney beans, undrained
1 (8 oz.) can whole kernel corn, undrained
1 (8 oz.) can tomato sauce
1 cup tomato juice
1 cup shredded cheddar cheese

Directions:

1. Heat Wok on high, add oil.
2. Stir fry onion, celery and zucchini for about 5 minutes.
3. Stir in powder, Worcestershire and ground red pepper.
4. Stir fry 1 minute.
5. Stir in beans, corn, tomato sauce, and tomato juice.
6. Bring to boil.
7. Reduce heat. Simmer uncovered about 10 minutes or until slightly thick. Serve and sprinkle cheese on top.

Caramel Corn

Ingredients:

1/2 cup brown sugar
1/2 cup (1 stick) butter
7 lg. marshmallows

Directions:

1. In electric non-stick wok on medium heat, stir brown sugar, butter and marshmallows.
2. Stir until marshmallows melt. Turn work off or unplug.
3. Pour 2 quarts popped popcorn into caramel sauce in wok and stir to mix until all corn is coated and cooled.

Stir Fry Turkey

Ingredients:

3/4 to 1 lb. raw skinless turkey breasts
Fresh parsley
Garlic
Onion
Mushrooms
3 to 4 oz. blush wine
1 chicken bouillon cube
3 to 4 carrots, scallion
Cornstarch

Directions:

1. Spray wok with Pam.
2. Add first 5 ingredients. Brown add wine 1 cup water, bouillon cube and carrots. Simmer 5 to 7 minutes. Thicken sauce with cornstarch and sprinkle scallion for garnish.
3. Serve with mashed potatoes, mashed with skin, milk and fresh peas or beans.

Wok Cole Slaw

Ingredients:

4 slices bacon, coarsely diced
1 cup walnuts
6 cup shredded red cabbage (1 med. cabbage)
1 med. yellow onion, thinly sliced
1 lg. apple, peeled and sliced
1/3 cup cider vinegar
2 tbsp. brown sugar
1/4 tsp. allspice
Salt and pepper to taste
Chopped parsley

Directions:

1. Heat wok over medium heat until it gets hot.
2. Add bacon and walnuts.
3. Stir-fry until bacon is crisp (about 2 minutes). Reserve two tbsps. of bacon fat. Discard the rest.
4. Add shredded cabbage and onion.
5. Stir-fry over high heat until cabbage begins to wilt (2 to 3 minutes).
6. Add apple vinegar, brown sugar and allspice.
7. Stir-fry until apple is cooked through (1 minute).
8. Season to taste with salt and pepper.
9. Sprinkle with chopped parsley. Serve immediately.

Wok Lasagna

Ingredients:

6 lasagna noodles, broken up (4 oz.)
1 cup cream style cottage cheese
4 oz. soft-style cream cheese
1/2 cup shredded Mozzarella cheese
1/2 cup shredded Mozzarella cheese
2 tbsp. grated Parmesan cheese
1/4 cup grated Parmesan cheese
1/2 tsp. Italian seasoning
3/4 lb. lean ground beef
1 clove garlic, minced
1 (15 1/2 oz.) jar spaghetti sauce with meat

Directions:

1. In a large saucepan, cook lasagna in boiling water for 10 to 12 minutes.
2. Drain and set aside.
3. In a medium mixing bowl, stir together cottage cheese, 1/2 cup Mozzarella cheese, 4 oz. cream cheese, 1/4 cup Parmesan cheese, and Italian seasoning. Set aside.
4. Preheat wok over high heat. Break up meat.
5. Stir fry meat and garlic for 2 to 3 minutes or until meat is brown. Spoon off fat.
6. Stir in spaghetti sauce and cooked noodles. Spoon cottage cheese mixture over mixture in Wok.
7. Sprinkle with 1/2 cup Mozzarella cheese, then Parmesan cheese.
8. Reduce heat.
9. Cover and cook about 5 minutes or until heated through.

Jalapeno Scallops And Plum Sauce

Ingredients:

16 lg. scallops
2 jalapenos, deseeded
1/8 cup candied ginger
1/8 cup white wine
1/8 cup plum sauce
1/8 lb. butter, unsalted
1 oz. soy sauce
1/2 cilantro bunch minced
1 clove garlic, minced
1 egg
1/8 cup corn starch

Directions:

1. Make a mixture of corn starch and water. Whip in one egg, add scallops. Then poach in boiling water for 2 minutes.
2. Remove scallops, discard corn starch water. Heat wok to medium heat, glaze with oil.
3. Add scallops, jalapenos, ginger, and garlic and stir fry for 30 seconds.
4. Add wine, plum sauce and soy sauce.
5. Reduce heat for 2 minutes, add butter and cilantro. Enjoy.

Sweet and Sour Chicken

Ingredients:

1 (8 oz.) can pineapple chunks, drained (juice reserved)
1/4 cup cornstarch
1 3/4 cups water, divided
3/4 cup white sugar
1/2 cup distilled white vinegar
2 drops orange food color
8 skinless, boneless chicken breast halves, cut into 1 inch cubes
2 1/4 cups self-rising flour
2 tbsps. vegetable oil
2 tbsps. cornstarch
1/2 tsp. salt
1/4 tsp. ground white pepper
1 egg
1 1/2 cups water
1 quart vegetable oil for frying
2 green bell pepper, cut into 1 inch pieces

Directions:

1. In a saucepan, combine 1 1/2 cups water, sugar, vinegar, reserved pineapple juice, and orange food coloring. Heat to boiling. Turn off heat.
2. Combine 1/4 cup cornstarch and 1/4 cup water; slowly stir into saucepan. Continue stirring until mixture thickens.
3. Combine flour, 2 tbsps. oil, 2 tbsps. cornstarch, salt, white pepper, and egg.
4. Add 1 1/2 cups water gradually to make a thick batter.
5. Stir to blend thoroughly.
6. Add chicken pieces, and stir until chicken is well coated.
7. Heat oil in wok to 360 degrees F (180 degrees C). Fry chicken pieces in hot oil 10 minutes, or until golden.
8. Remove chicken, and drain on paper towels.
9. When ready to serve, layer green peppers, pineapple chunks, and cooked chicken pieces on a platter.
10. Pour hot sweet and sour sauce over top.

About the Author

Laura Sommers is **The Recipe Lady!**

She is a loving wife and mother who lives on a small farm in Baltimore County, Maryland and has a passion for all things domestic especially when it comes to saving money. She has a profitable eBay business and is a couponing addict. Follow her tips and tricks to learn how to make delicious meals on a budget, save money or to learn the latest life hack!

Thank you for purchasing this book. I hope that you enjoyed all the delicious recipes. If you enjoyed this book, please take a moment to leave a review. Reviews help with the sale of the book and help me to support my family. Thank you for your kindness.

Visit her Amazon Author Page to see her latest books:

amazon.com/author/laurasommers

Visit the Recipe Lady's blog for even more great recipes:

http://the-recipe-lady.blogspot.com/

Follow the Recipe Lady on **Pinterest**:

http://pinterest.com/therecipelady1

Other Books by Laura Sommers

Egg Salad Recipes

The Chip Dip Cookbook

Zucchini Recipes

Salsa recipes

Traditional Vermont Recipes

Recipe Hacks for Dry Onion Soup Mix

Manufactured by Amazon.ca
Bolton, ON

15143910R00058